Notes For The Last Kind Ones

David Teahan

© 2025 Farbellum Press. All rights reserved.

No part of this publication may be reproduced, stored in a retrieval system, or transmitted in any form or by any means: electronic, mechanical, photocopying, recording, or otherwise, without the prior written permission of the publisher, except in the case of brief quotations used in reviews or critical articles.

This is a work of nonfiction. All reflections are based on lived experience, general observation, and personal insight. While care has been taken to ensure accuracy and sensitivity, this book is not intended as professional advice.

First edition, 2025

ISBN: Paperback: 978-1-7641306-3-9 eBook: 978-1-7641306-4-6

Cover design and formatting by Farbellum Press

Published by Farbellum Press, Written by David Teahan

www.farbellum.com

Table of Contents

Introduction 1

Part I The Belonging We Forgot: When a Person Was Enough

You Aren't Alone. We All Are. 5

The Checklist That Didn't Include Breathing 12

You Are Not Behind. You're Just Tired. 21

You Carry More Than You Know 25

Some Days You're the Plant. Some Days You're the Sunlight. ... 32

Ritual is a Memory You Can Touch 35

The Quiet Ones Aren't Broken 42

Self-Help for the Kind Ones: 30 Quiet Acts of Survival 44

Part II The Hollowing: What We Lost While We Optimised

The Day Your Job Became Your Identity 49

The Age of Constant Comparison 55

The Myth of Emotional Capitalism 65

Human Dignity Vs Market Logic 70

What Can't Be Automated (Yet) 75

The Subscription Self 79

Presence for Sale 82

The Algorithm of Belonging 85

When Work Became Content 87

The Last Meaningful Gesture 89

Part III The Return: What We Remembered

Refusing the Performance 93

Stillness in a Monetised World 96

Living Beyond the Feed 99

The Soul Beyond Usefulness 102

What They Can't Take From You 105

You Don't Have to Be the Glue 108

Quiet Enough for the Wind to Speak 115

Letters to the Ones Still Trying 118

Books For the Quiet Return 121

Introduction

Have you ever just sat beneath a tree on a warm autumn afternoon, watching the leaves drift by? Has it been a while? That's okay. For most of us, it happens less these days.

Because right now something is happening that keeps us from moments like that. The world is being automated, optimised, and flattened into content. Algorithms are deciding what we see, what we value, even how we think.

Kindness is becoming a novelty. Rest is seen as laziness. And in the middle of it all, too many people feel like they're quietly fading from the unbearable pressure of it all.

But it doesn't have to end this way. This can still be the beginning of something quieter. Something more human. A renewal.

This isn't just a collection of words. These pages weren't thrown together by an AI or stitched from recycled internet posts. They were written with soul, and intention, from one of you.

From one of the Last Kind Ones.

Because if you found this book, I already know it's for you. Call it chance, fate, or just a strange little miracle.

The world we live in makes us tired. The kind of tired no sleep can fix. No amount of sugary snacks or mindless scrolling can solve it. But what can? Focusing again on what is important.

If you've ever looked up at the night sky or even at your plain white ceiling, and wondered if maybe it's not you that's broken, but the world around you… You're not alone.

There are millions of us. The Last Kind Ones. The quiet builders. Builders not of skyscrapers or computer code. But builders of hope, truth, and moments of real connection. Even now, when those feel like endangered species or remnants of a time gone by.

This book exists because the modern world hums too loudly. It moves too fast, and leaves too many of us feeling empty. The kind ones are burning out quietly. Many are surrendering to the pace, believing they don't have a choice. We're told to hustle, to optimize, to produce. Go here. Get this. Do more. Share it. Perform it. And yet no one teaches us how to stay soft, how to remain human, how to breathe.

But this book is here to say: you can.

You can build hope. You can be tender and tired. You can care deeply and still feel overwhelmed. You're not failing. You're just not being seen. But I see you. And so do all the other Last Kind Ones.

So, who is this book for? The overthinkers. The tired hearts. The people who still send "let me know when you get home safe" texts. The ones who check in on others while quietly falling apart themselves. The digital wanderers, roaming what's left of the internet, looking for something that still feels real in a sea of fake.

This book genre does not help at times either. These days, self-help has become less of a genre and more of a religion. For many, just owning the book is supposed to fix it all; as if placing it on the shelf will summon magical transformation from some wizard. But no book can do everything. Especially not the ones calling themselves self-help that yell at you to try harder, wake up earlier, do more with less. As if you, personally, are the problem.

This book isn't here to shame you into changing. It's here to sit beside you while you remember how much you've already survived. There is advice here and it's not the kind that requires 14-hour days or a fake online persona. It's gentle, practical, and meant for real lives.

Read what you can, when you can. No pressure. Keep it close; on your nightstand, in your bag, or as a quiet companion on the bus. And when you see someone sitting alone in the park, that person you pass every day but never speak to; consider giving them a copy. They might need it too.

But more than advice, I want you to know this: you are not alone. And if that's all these pages manage to say, well, that's a beautiful thing.

You weren't meant to carry it all alone. You aren't meant to feel like you do. You don't need it. Not the pressure. Not the pace. Not the performance.

Let's walk slowly now, through the noise and we will try and remember what was real before the world forgot.

Part I
The Belonging We Forgot:
When a Person Was Enough

You Aren't Alone. We All Are.

Let's talk about loneliness and being alone. There are nights when the silence is proof no one called rather than a relaxing respite from the noise.

Maybe you're one of the lucky ones. Surrounded by warmth, tangled in a household of affection, a recast Brady Bunch with better lighting and lo-fi playlists.

Maybe your phone buzzes with invitations, your evenings full of laughter, movie nights, and story-swapping with people who remember your dog's name and your star sign.

But probably not. Because statistically that's very few of us these days. Most people are lonely now.

And those people who live in the golden glow of effortless connection rarely buy books like this. They're probably busy training for Everest or planning a group trip to Tuscany because life is just too abundant (please bring me back some wine!).

We are the many. The uninvited. The half-heard. The ones who answer "How are you?" with a nod and a smile and a quiet ache when we notice it not asked back.

We don't wear badges. We don't signal to each other (although how cool would secret society signals be?!). We walk past each other in the street wearing the same armour: societally acceptable clothes, a face of pleasant half smile, eyes aimed at the middle distance. But inside? Inside, we're tired. And alone.

And I'm here to tell you that's okay. Not just because I feel it too, but because there are reasons. Real ones. It's not your fault. Not some character flaw or broken morning routine. You didn't need to splash your face with mineral water fourteen times.

Let's start with a definition. Merriam-Webster (who sound terribly important) defines loneliness as "being without company; separated from others". But that doesn't cut it. Not here. Because loneliness isn't about company, it's about connection. You can be surrounded by people and still feel like a ghost in the crowd.

Western society has mastered the slow art of isolation. Covid just sped things up. It was a crazy time and I feel we all still have a little bit of PTSD from it. Offices closed. Kitchen tables became work desks. The little social friction of everyday life that included hellos in hallways, bad coffee in break rooms, disappeared. And when employers realised it saved money? That model stayed. Nothing drives societal change quicker than profit.

We accepted it, too. We embraced it even. Less commuting, more flexibility. We saw it as an opportunity to see family more maybe, for those with children at home. On paper, it was a win. But in reality? It frayed the thin threads we didn't even know were holding us together.

Add to that the rise of social media. More connection than ever. And somehow, less intimacy. Everyone a broadcast. Everyone a brand. Scrolling through highlight reels while eating dinner alone.

Our social distance in person creates our siloed nature online, where echo chambers repeat our views and an algorithm pushes us further into a define category.

Then families shrank. Birth rates continue to fall. Friends moved cities. Community dissolved into convenience.

And here we are.

Now, no one's twirling a moustache behind a curtain causing this. There is no one pulling the invisible strings. No gigantic secret society to blame. It's just momentum. Economics. Urban sprawl. Cultural shift. And a terribly bad convergence of multiple factors that have led us to be drifting. Drifting far from what it means to be human.

Therapists will tell you to join a club. Find a hobby group. Attend a workshop. Learn Skiing in a desert, or whatever the cool kids are doing. Because a text book told them to say that. But that same therapist probably goes home, drinks a bottle of wine while watching episodes of Friends and crying because they aren't coping either.

Maybe you don't want to do their recommendations, or to play Scrabble with strangers at the community hall while a guy called Bob steals all the pieces (*looking at you Bob*). Maybe you just want one person to call who gets you. Not fix you. Not network with you. Just sit in the same silence.

Because that's what most of us crave. Not activity. Not productivity. But presence.

Real connection doesn't require a workshop or a community hall. Sometimes it's as simple as a phone call. Let me tell you a story.

One of my best friends called last week. He lives two hundred kilometres away. I hadn't seen him in three months. He wanted to talk.

I should have been thrilled. But he called right after work, and my brain was still chewing through a to-do list. Emails to respond to. Dinner to prep. The looming sense that if I didn't hustle hard enough, the world would close one more door.

As he told me about feeling down, starting therapy, about the side effects of a medication, I found myself drifting. Glancing at my screen. Thinking about everything waiting for me, the pressure of things to complete and the fear of falling behind. Hoping, guiltily, that he'd wrap it up.

Twenty minutes later, I ended the call and felt awful. That was someone I loved. And I had watched the clock during the conversation. But for many of us this is what modern connection has become. Fragmented. Scheduled. Transactional.

We talk in bullet points. We listen in fragments. We've been trained by TikTok, by hustle culture, by email pings and algorithmic outrage to prefer speed over depth. And sadness? Real sadness? It's slow. It doesn't trend.

So, we shrink our emotional lives down to soundbites. We ghost each other not out of malice, but from overload; choosing the treadmill of our fast-paced society over compassion, afraid that stopping might cost us something in a world that rewards only momentum.

And when we do make time, we're often too tired to be fully present.

Take work for example. Hustle isn't a choice anymore; it's a survival tactic. I'm not chasing protein shakes and 3am gym sessions. I'm chasing enough money to stay afloat. To save for something. Anything. And still, it's a struggle to do that.

Our senses are overloaded. Emails, ads, texts, endless news cycles. Even the gentle voice of a friend becomes just one more sound in a noisy day. And the longer we delay those check-ins with each other, pushing them aside for the god of productivity, the lonelier we all become.

And the guilt builds.

Because kind people know. We feel it when we let someone down, even when we had nothing left to give. We feel the hurt, see it in their eyes, sense it in the silence. Empathy is a double-edged sword, and it swings wildly in the face of modern life.

But it's not our fault. We're adapting to an insane environment. And we're doing the best we can.

The irony? The lonelier we feel, the more likely we are to act in ways that deepen that loneliness. Missing calls. Ignoring messages. Retreating into tasks. It becomes a self-fulfilling pattern, but that doesn't make it permanent. It just means we have to fight a little harder to break it (This would be a great time to cue *Eye of the Tiger* on the playlist).

Let me time-travel for a second. Picture the 1970s. Awful fashion. Strange food. A tragic overuse of beige. But also: connection. People went places after work. They talked. They laughed. They overcooked microwave pork roasts at fondue parties hosted by neighbours wearing aggressively knitted jumpers, drinking beer that required a can opener.

The television used to sit across the room like a lazy pet. It didn't follow you everywhere. It didn't fit in your pocket. And when you gathered with friends, you weren't also checking seventeen tabs or receiving constant notifications trying to drive up your engagement.

Now, a two-hour phone-free dinner with friends feels like a revolutionary act, as if suddenly you are causing the downfall of the Russian Czar all over again. And that's wild. Because it shouldn't be.

Sharing a meal. Making eye contact. Being truly present, these were once ordinary things. Now they feel like rebellion. Like pushing back against the current.

We didn't choose this shift. No one voted for this. It crept in slowly. It started with a quick glance at a screen. A reply mid-conversation. A buzz that breaks the silence. Until even our moments of connection started to fracture.

It can start with something as simple as putting the phone down and saying: "I'm here. Fully. Wearing a knitted jumper."

We shouldn't feel like revolutionaries in the jungles of Ecuador just for wanting real, non-digital face-to-face conversation.

And can we stop asking what someone does for work within one minute of meeting them? Please? That's not identity. That's branding.

Trust also affects our connection to others. We don't even trust each other anymore. Not really. Social trust is low. Not because we're bad (well your cat is, but we're not here to judge); but because we have been burned. By banks. By politics. By those we gave our hearts to.

We're all a little heartbroken. Twice-divorced, even if we've never married. A collection of country songs just without the chart-topping success.

What do we do? We start small.

Find one person. Propose a movie night. Phones off. Real popcorn.

Feeling bolder? Organise a dinner. No one cooks. No one cleans. Fried chicken, laughter, and eye contact.

That's how we rebuild, one meal at a time. One conversation without multitasking. One quiet fireside chat.

And if that feels like too much? That's okay too.

To the one who is truly alone; no nearby friends, no calls, no plans. You, who moved countries, changed jobs, or simply drifted from your roots; you are not forgotten.

You aren't alone. We all are.
And nothing stays still forever.

In the meantime, be kind to yourself Goddammit.

The Checklist That Didn't Include Breathing

They gave you a job title, a desk, and a string of tasks. But they forgot to leave you a place to breathe.

Maybe you bought a small plant. Something green and struggling under fluorescent lights. Or taped up a photo of your kids at the beach, only to be told by management that personal items were "discouraged because they make the office look untidy."

The desk was grey. The walls were grey. And after a few weeks, something in you started to feel that way too.

Somewhere along the line, the world confused motion with meaning.
We started to measure our worth in clicks, emails, calendar invites, and unread notifications. Your manager did too, not by the kindness in your voice or the integrity of your choices, but by the number of tasks you could juggle without dropping.

Our lives became spreadsheets. Colour-coded. Optimised. Prioritised. Whole hours pass now rearranging the very tasks we never had time to question in the first place.

Processes multiplied. Reports justified their own existence. Before long, the job wasn't to move things forward but it was to sustain the illusion that we were meant to be doing any of this at all. Work, for the sake of work.

I once knew a workplace where managers were tasked with opening a report, copying its contents into a new report, and presenting it to executives as if it were new. The information already existed. The executives could have accessed it themselves.

But the task had become theatre. A ritual. Like the emperor demanding grapes that were peeled and arranged on a golden platter by a chain of middle managers. It was performance masquerading as productivity. And we all played along, because questioning the ritual felt more dangerous than doing it.

And quietly, in the process, our lungs forgot how to fully expand.

You wake not to sunlight, but to a buzzing slab of glass telling you what you missed. Messages. Meetings. A breakfast you won't eat.

You shuffle into the day already behind. You check your email before you brush your teeth. You apologise for not replying. You reply anyway, even when there's nothing left in you.

Because modern work doesn't ask how you are. It asks how soon.

There's a particular kind of exhaustion that comes not from lifting, but from repeating. Click here. Approve that. Forward this. Log that.

You end the day having done a hundred things, and somehow still wonder if you accomplished anything real.

This is the kind of work that has evolved without meaning:

Processes for the sake of process.

Emails in response to emails.

Meetings to prepare for meetings.

We have built whole job roles that orbit abstract goals and floating objectives, divorced from anything tangible.

And we feel it; deep down, even if we never say it out loud: I am tired of pretending this is what I was meant to do.

I am tired of trying to portray this job as meaningful.

I am tired of putting my soul into spreadsheets and calling it purpose.

I am tired of finding new ways to make the pointless look polished and professional.

Let's talk about those endless emails. The ones that loop in four extra people just to confirm something no one cares about. The ones where *"did you see my last message"* is a polite way to scream into the void; or it's your inner passive-aggressive work monster clawing its way out.

Entire careers are now built on digital echoes of a long-lost spreadsheet god; approving, refining, reformatting things that will never exist outside a PowerPoint slide.

You're not launching rockets, Damian in Accounts. Chill out.
You're realigning bullet points.
And somehow, that takes all day.

We've created a strange reward system.

One where people get promoted not for results, but for appearing indispensable. The ones who make their struggles visible. Stay late enough to appear to be martyrs. And wear their exhaustion like a badge of honour.

There is a poetic irony in that; a system that claims to reward performance ends up promoting performance art.

Theatrics over substance. Exhaustion as proof of dedication.

There's something broken in that.

We once valued hands in soil; effort that left fingerprints. Now we value keystrokes more. But not all work is equal, and not all jobs were meant to alienate us from the feeling of having made something.

White-collar work promised us comfort. Climate control. Lanyards. Free coffee. A view. A back free from pain.
But too often, it delivered abstraction. Disconnection. The strange sensation of living your life inside a PDF document.

Many of us haven't touched the real outcome of our labour in years.

Physical work may exhaust the body, but it rarely forgets the soul. There's dignity in fixing, building, delivering. In handing something over and saying, "I made this". In standing beside a wall you helped paint, or a table you helped craft; even if it wobbles a little.

Compare that to… closing another tab. Meeting another KPI. Losing another hour to an email that could've been silence.

Now, I'm not saying we all need to become carpenters - trust me on this one I should confess: my own brief brush with manual labour was, well, humbling.
During woodworking in school, I once designed a birdhouse so small no bird could enter, and a wheel that was, quite proudly, square. It wobbled like a metaphor for my future in manual labour.

Let's just say I did not miss my hidden calling, and neither did it miss me. My woodworking teacher probably startles at the sound of sandpaper due to the PTSD I caused them.

And speaking of KPIs (key performance indicators) let's be honest: they are often the antithesis of human connection.
When your job is to answer forty-seven calls an hour, how much space is left to care?
How much room is there for kindness, for patience, for depth? The metric becomes the master, and the person on the other end becomes someone to battle against, to get off the phone as quickly as possible.

And maybe you've been on both sides.
You've sent the rushed email. You've ignored the human in favour of the metric. So have I. We're not villains; we're just tired and trying. Following the rules we were told mattered. Until something in us started whispering that maybe, just maybe, they don't.

Of course, the world needs both the white and the blue collar. The coder and the courier. The planner and the gardener. But something's tilted too far. Our culture rewards image over substance. Meetings over meaning. It whispers, constantly: Don't rest. Don't slow. Don't breathe.

Maybe you've felt it. That slow panic as the to-do list at work grows. The creeping guilt for not working late, not taking on that one more thing. The way some of us, even on weekends, feel the ghost-tap of an email notification that isn't there.

So, you take the laptop to the couch. You nod through the Teams call. You answer messages while stirring a pot of pasta, glancing toward your child who just asked a question you didn't quite hear. Two tasks at once. And somewhere in all that, you forget how silence feels. How freedom feels. How doing nothing feels.

But here's the secret: you are allowed to do nothing.

You are allowed to let the dishes sit. You are allowed to take a walk without earbuds. You are allowed to take another path.

Have you ever noticed how someone doing nothing feels vaguely unsettling now? As if they're breaking an unspoken law. The stranger on the beach just staring at the waves. The woman on a park bench watching the wind move through trees. The man standing still in a car park, head tilted toward the sky.

We used to call that presence. Now we treat it like a glitch in the matrix. Like they are the weird ones.

When did we start to fear those who slowed down? As if they are the problem in this world? They're not.

There are movements rising in response to this. In China, some call it "*lying flat*"; a quiet protest against hustle, against a life spent proving your usefulness at work. In the West, we name it burnout. We build apps to soothe it. After all, is it really mindfulness if you don't have a journaling app with a pastel-coloured interface, a seven-day streak badge, and a push notification reminding you to be present?

We put it on mugs. But at its core is the same aching truth:

We were not designed to live this way.

And here's something powerful: you can still play the game, without letting it own you. You can still reply to the email. You can still nod politely at the colleague who makes everything harder.

But deep down, you can realise what they don't: none of this defines you.

Not your job title. Not your meeting. Not your efficiency ranking. You are not a human spreadsheet. You are a person. And your worth isn't in what you produce, it's in how you show up. How you soften. How you care for others.

You don't have to quit your job or move to the mountains. You can start with something smaller: a moment. A boundary. A decision not to apologise for logging off.

Or you can:

Let the meeting flow. Don't pour your energy into a decision you don't control.

Know their motivation: that annoying manager may just be doing that because their manager told them to. They are human too.

Always think it through. Before you send that snappy email, pause. Give it an hour. A night. Let clarity come first.

Don't let the invisible forces of the office force your pace. Running 10 percent slower is not going to cause the downfall of civilization.

You can still do your tasks. Still send your emails. Still be polite to the colleague who tests your soul, and quite possibly is the reincarnation of some ancient force of evil. But you can also carry this quiet knowledge: they do not own your attention.

Your value is not measured in response time. Your legacy will not be built in shared drives. Your kindness matters more than your KPIs.

At your funeral, no one will stand up to praise how promptly you replied to emails. They will talk about how you made them feel. About that one moment you paused to listen. Or helped them keep their sanity when the world felt too much.

We're not failing.

We're adapting.

Some days that means rising.

Other days, it means resisting quietly by remembering we are still human beneath the metrics.

Let yourself breathe.

And if you do happen to be working with the reincarnation of the devil itself, eventually they will realise the error of their ways. Most likely when they are 80, angry, looking in the mirror and thinking "why was I such a dick".

You Are Not Behind. You're Just Tired.

There is a voice inside you; faint, but there. It says: "I should be doing more".

It whispers this while you're brushing your teeth. While you're trying to enjoy a quiet coffee. While you're scrolling past other people's milestones, promotions, travels, and photo-worthy productivity. You start to feel like life is a race and everyone else was given a head start.

That they picked the right degree.
They moved to the right city. Met the right person.
That they knew something you didn't.

And now, you're stuck in the version of a life that wasn't supposed to happen. The parallel timeline. The lesser one. You wonder if every small choice, every pause, every risk not taken, added up to this. This quiet sense of being behind. After all that's what the books and the social media posts have told you. It's your fault, right?

But here's the part the algorithm never shows you: Everyone feels like that sometimes. Even the people whose lives you scroll past.

You need to know. You are not behind. You're just tired.

Tired from carrying expectations that were never yours.
Tired from deadlines stacked like bricks on your spine.
Tired from surviving things you never got credit for surviving.
You have not fallen behind. You have moved forward under conditions that would have made many stop.

Let's talk about the myth of the universal timeline. School by this age. Career by that one. Partnered. Mortgage. Two kids. A passport full of stamps. Savings. Muscles. Mindfulness. By thirty, if possible. Earlier, if you're truly exceptional.

These timelines were built for no one in particular, by people you'll never meet, shaped by markets, media, and marketing departments that want you to feel behind so you'll keep consuming, keep comparing, keep proving your worth by what you produce. They want you to feel bad. That makes you a buyer.

Always remember, those who seem to have it all are often carrying more darkness than we will ever know. They hurt too, they've just mastered the angle, the caption, the filter. Pain doesn't disappear when it's well-lit.

Your tiredness is not laziness. It's not failure. It's the sign of a soul worn thin by noise, by pressure, by the weight of pretending it's all fine. Maybe it's time to honour that tiredness. Maybe it's time to stop measuring your life in the speed it runs by but rather in your presence in the moment.

You are not a slow version of someone else. You are the first version of you. Sometimes your progress is quiet, unseen, internal. But that doesn't make it any less real.

And let's not forget the world we've been in. A world that spun off its axis. The pandemic, the political upheavals, the economic tremors, the social media noise, the pressure to have an opinion on everything, the sheer overstimulation of it all.

Now more than ever, there's a feeling in the air that time, for perhaps the first time in human history, is collectively running out.

Not just personal time, not just your deadlines, your goals, but time itself.

As if something irreversible has already been set in motion. As if we're all subconsciously holding our breath, waiting for a future that feels more like a countdown than a horizon.

A quiet urgency hums beneath everything now. A wall of pressure building, that we cannot see but feel. As if something larger is shifting. As if the world, knowingly or not, is bracing for a change that has not yet arrived, but will.

If through this urgency and pressure you've managed to simply stay kind, you are not behind; you are remarkable.

You've had days where you got out of bed and faced the world, even when you didn't want to.

You've had moments where you listened to a friend when you had nothing left. You've shown up to jobs, family dinners, group chats, and life itself while holding things no one else could see.

You have not failed.

You have adapted.

There will be more chapters. More time. You are not late. You are on a path that doesn't look like theirs; and that's because it's yours.

Let yourself rest.

Let yourself be enough.

Let the seasons unfold without needing to harvest something from every single one.

You are not behind.
You're just tired.
And you are allowed to breathe.

You Carry More Than You Know

An opening for the Poets

You do not walk alone.

Even when the room is empty. Even when the streetlight flickers to darkness and the path ahead narrows.

There are hands on your shoulders you cannot see, echoes in your bones you've never noticed, weight in your chest that does not belong to this soul.

You carry more than you know.

Maybe no one ever told you this. Maybe you've spent your life wondering why you tire so easily, why joy arrives like an abrupt short chorus instead of a song.

But the truth is this: some of what you feel isn't just yours.

It belongs to the ones who came before you; the ones who never got the chance to put it down.
The battles they fought.
The tragedies they overcame.
The quiet hopes they never voiced.
Intergenerational trauma.

They live on in us; not as burdens, but as echoes.

The Inheritance of Weight

Across generations, we inherit more than hairlines and eye colours. We inherit silence. We inherit coping mechanisms. We inherit the smell of fear. The rhythm of war drums. We inherit the talent for dying on the inside without making a scene.

You may be the grandchild of someone who never had time to heal. Who was taught to endure, not feel. Who believed survival was enough; and maybe, for them, it was.

But you? You are trying to live.

And that's harder. Because now, the weight has shifted. You're not just carrying their dreams. You're carrying their disappointments. Their worn beliefs. Their unspoken prayers.

It's a quiet burden. The kind that doesn't announce itself. It shows up in the moments you freeze before making a decision; our ancestral fight-or-flight rising like smoke. It stirs in the guilt you feel for resting, as if someone long gone is whispering in your ear.

We flinch at stillness. We over-explain. We wonder if we are too much, or not enough.

Some of what you carry is not yours. But it still asks to be carried like an unnamed weight. That is our unspoken inheritance. A story half-told in the silence between generations.

None of us are born free of this weight. But naming it gently, honestly, is how we begin to set it down.

The Rhythms We Lost

We were meant to live by starlight.

Our ancestors didn't just survive the dark; they made peace with it. They gathered around fires, shared bread and myth and silence. They told stories not to go viral, but to stay human. To connect.

There was a direct, deeper connection then. Every glance at the night sky reminded them of the vastness above and the grounding below. To live in rhythm with the moon and the seasons was not aesthetic; it was survival, and it was soul.

You weren't fighting the world's presence; you were part of it. Feet on soil. Heart in tune. Light came from flame, not from screens. Warmth came from bodies, not settings on a dial.

Today we live beneath fluorescents, surrounded by the glow of screens and the blink of surveillance cameras; and increasingly, drones. Even in rest, we are watched. Even in stillness, we are expected to produce.

Our rhythms used to be lunar, seasonal, sacred. Now they are algorithmic.

We sleep too late. Wake too early. Eat while working. Scroll while eating. Respond before thinking. Reply before feeling We move so fast, we don't even notice we're lost. Until we are many miles from our intended destination.

We Forget to sit by the campfire. The firelight is gone, replaced by the cold hue of productivity. But somewhere in us, the old

rhythms remain; quiet, but not dead.
They wait for us in the moments we sit without distraction.
In the instinct to light a candle.
In the pause before answering.
In the moment we stand in the shower just that bit extra to feel.
In the ache for a slower, truer life.

You carry their memory even now.

And some part of you remembers how it felt to be warm beside the fire, surrounded not by noise, but by people laughing. Not by comment threads, but by stories and love. Not by competition, but by communion.

The ache you feel isn't failure.
It's the ancient part of you, wondering what happened to the life you were meant for.
The life we were all meant for.

The Myth of the Self-Made Person

We are told to be self-made. That success comes from grit, hustle, a never-ending devotion to becoming someone new. But that story erases the truth: you are not a solo act.

You are made of everyone who ever believed in you, and everyone who didn't. You are shaped by the lullabies sung to your ancestors, the migrations of people and the mistakes, the shared meals and survival stories passed down like sacred code.

You are the result of everything endured, everything loved, everything let go of.

There is no such thing as a self-made person. Only self-aware ones; those who know they stand on the shoulders of others, and bow in gratitude for it.

The myth of individualism is seductive. It sells well, it's profitable to companies. It flatters the ego. It fits neatly into hustle culture. It gives false hope that you, alone, like a lighthouse, can thrive. But it isolates the soul.
Because when you think you're supposed to do it all on your own, you forget to ask for help. You forget that community was the original safety net.

You carry more than you know. But not all of it is meant to be carried alone.

Breaking the Line

Some of us were born to break the pattern. To end the silence. To stop pretending everything's fine. To feel what others buried. But it comes at a cost.

If you are the first to go to therapy, the first to say "that stops with me", the first to choose gentleness over power, you are doing sacred work. And it's exhausting.

It is emotionally draining doing what those before you could not. You are not just living your life; you're untangling generations of quiet sorrow. You're rewriting your journey, without a map.

Healing, unlike the experience of hurt, is slow. Softening takes more strength than becoming jaded. To forgive, to pause, to speak when silence has ruled for decades, these are not small acts. They are revolutions.

It mattered. You mattered.
And you broke the line, so others could walk free.

And one day, someone will thank you for being the first.
Even if they never know your name.
Even if they never see the cracks you sealed with your own hands.
Even if your work was invisible, the freedom it gave won't be.

You are not alone. There are millions of us; quiet, kind, and carrying more than we show. Builders of something gentler, rising from the rubble of whatever this society has become. Dreamers of a kinder way.

Reclaiming Culture as Soul

Culture isn't a content strategy. It's not a fashion trend, or a hashtag, or a marketing pitch.

It's a song your grandmother sang while cooking. It's the carved bowl passed from one hand to another. It's the stories that began with "Back in my day…" and ended in knowing laughter. It's rituals, language, spice, scent. It's the sorrow, the joy, and the steady core of who you are.

We were not meant to consume culture. We were meant to carry it.

Capitalism turns identity into a marketplace. It asks: What part of you can be monetised? What traditions can be trademarked? What grief can be sold as aesthetic?

But you are not a brand. You are a body, a breath, a becoming.

To reclaim culture is to reject performance. It is to gather without posting. To cook without photographing. To honour the quiet, sacred acts that make you remember who you were before you were marketed to. Your soul is not a business model. Let it be fed, not packaged.

A Reflective Close

We were meant to live by starlight, not security light.

To gather by fire, not flicker.

To measure life not in clicks, but in closeness.

There is so much you carry. But there is also so much you've already laid down. So much you've let go of. So much you've healed quietly, in the dark, with no applause.

You are the memory and the maker. The heir and the healer. The echo and the answer.

You are carried. And you carry too.

But you are not alone.

We are the Last Kind Ones. And we are with you.

Some Days You're the Plant. Some Days You're the Sunlight.

There are days you bloom. And days you barely breathe. Both are sacred.

The world taught you to perform, to produce, to peak on cue. To treat energy like a resource to be mined, not a rhythm to be honoured. But you are not a machine.

You are a living thing. A changing thing. A being, not a business.

And just like plants, you have your seasons.

Some days you stretch toward the light, embracing those around you. You feel joy in your bones. You text people back. You remember to drink water. You're soft and open and easy to love.

Other days, you're roots. You're underground. Gathering. Quiet. Still. Secure in the soil. Not dead, just hidden. Healing. Preparing. Waiting for the next warmth to arrive.

The miracle is: both are necessary.

We are not meant to be sunlight all the time. We are not meant to fake joy or hustle through every moment. Leave that to the court jesters of old. Growth doesn't always look like motion. Healing doesn't always look like progress. Sometimes it's just not falling apart.

Sometimes, it looks like sitting still in your pyjamas from the previous night, un-showered, wondering what the point is.

Sometimes its tears for no reason, or naps that don't fix the tiredness but somehow make you feel more drained, as if the very weight of your mind was expressed in your dreams. Sometimes it's disappearing from the world just to remember who you are without the world watching.

Across cultures and centuries, rest was once revered; not something to be earned after exhaustion, but something embedded in the rhythm of life. The Sabbath. The siesta. The silent tea rituals in Japan. The unhurried meals under banyan trees in Indonesia. These were not acts of laziness. They were acknowledgements that being human required rest, not just speed.

In many Indigenous communities, storytelling took place at dusk; when no one was working, and the land was still.
That pause was not wasted time; it was soul time.
And in those pauses, wisdom landed deeper than any lecture or performance ever could.

We've forgotten these ancestral agreements. Capitalism didn't just sell us things; it stole our tempo. With no money back guarantee.

You don't have to justify your quiet days. Or your sad days. Or your dark days where you attack everyone via email as if you are launching a new crusade. Rest is not a reward. And worth is not a currency.

Some days you'll feel like the sunshine in someone else's life. Supporting them and bringing them the strength they need. Other days, you'll need their warmth just to get out of bed. Both roles are real. Both are worthy.

Let yourself be cyclical. Let yourself be weathered. Let yourself be alive.

Some days you're the plant. Some days you're the sunlight.

And on many days, you're just doing your best to stay rooted.

That is enough.

It always was.

Ritual is a Memory You Can Touch

Evening settles gently over a narrow side street in Hội An, just beyond the tourist lanes with their lanterns and laughter.
Here, in the quieter part of town, a family gathers at a low table set just inside the threshold of their home.
The door remains open to the dusk. A breeze carries in the scent of grilled lemongrass, the faint whine of a motorbike disappearing into the distance, and the soft clink of bowls being placed by practiced hands.

They've all worked today; the parents, the older son, even the grandmother, who still insists on buying the herbs herself each morning. Their clothes are simple, mostly a mix of overstock designs once destined for export, now sold locally at market stalls. Their bodies are tired; but as they sit, their faces soften.

No one rushes. There is no background television. No endless scroll of glowing rectangles. Just the flow of the meal being prepared, and the prayer that precedes it.

The youngest child clasps her hands together, peeking one eye open at her mother beside her. The father bows his head, murmuring thanks not to a deity of power, but of provision. Gratitude for rice, for fish sauce, for the company of those still here.

They do not say it aloud, but every plate laid is a reminder of those no longer at the table, and of the quiet love passed down in recipes and repetition.

There is nothing performative here. No audience. No livestream. No photos for an update.

It is not grand.

But it is real.

And that is enough.

The Quiet Strength of Culture

There are cultures where elders are still greeted with bowed heads, not eye-rolls. Where food is not plated in silence, but shared across generations. Where birthdays are less about presents and more about presence.

In these cultures, ritual is not some distant artifact. It is alive; stitched into the everyday. It's in the incense lit at sunrise. The bowl of fruit placed before an ancestor's photo. The weekend market where three generations argue over herbs and haggle like poetry.

Much of what we now call 'balance' or 'wellness' is simply what other cultures never unlearned.

Family dinners. Sacred holidays. Slowness. Prayer before meals. Chores done together, not alone. A walk to the temple. A kiss to the hand of an elder.

The modern world continues its encroachment. Far from its Western origins, it now reaches even the quiet corners of the earth and sees these things differently. Rituals are framed as optional, not essential. But for many cultures, they are the heartbeat of meaning.

Even the rise of the digital nomad tells us something. It's not just about freedom or Wi-Fi by the beach. It's an ache. A reaching. A quiet recognition that something is missing in our fast, fragmented lives. Many young people aren't just running from office cubicles; they're running toward something ancient. Because the office cubicles of today are not those of twenty years ago. So, they move toward street food, shared laughter, community meals. Toward places where elders are still honoured, and joy is still cooked daily in open-air kitchens.

To reclaim this kind of culture doesn't require a passport. You can begin with small rituals. A candle lit with intention. A meal eaten without screens. A story told from memory instead of a device.

You don't need to be religious either. You just need to be willing to remember.

Ritual is remembrance. Culture is grounding. The sacred doesn't owe you an explanation.

Culture Isn't a Performance

Culture was never meant to be curated. It is not a costume. Not a mood board. Not a clever tweet about your "aesthetic," or whether it matches your IKEA furniture.

Culture is what holds us; not what we hold up for display.

Somewhere along the way, many of us became performers of our own heritage. We posted our dishes but forgot their origin stories. We wore pieces of tradition without knowing the names of the hands that stitched them. We filled our homes with relics from past generations as if display could replace connection; imitating what we stopped reaching inside to feel. We spoke of roots without remembering the soil.

But culture doesn't ask to be performed through photos on social media. It asks to be lived.

You don't need to be fluent in your ancestral language to honour it. There's something profoundly tender in the laughter around a table when, never having spoken the language before, you attempt it anyway; a conversation of gestures, smiles, and effort. That too is a form of remembering.

You don't need to know every myth or every recipe. What matters is the sincerity with which you show up; to remember, to reclaim, to reconnect.

To walk through the market and greet the elders in your awkward accent.
To call your aunt and ask how your grandmother used to make that dish.
To light a candle and whisper thanks, even if the name you speak for the divine has changed.

You are allowed to begin again.

You are allowed to return home.
Even if your family left it behind three generations ago.
Even if your ancestors were forced across oceans without their

consent.
Your soul is still partly there.
Because you still feel it.
You are still connected.
And some part of you never left.
Even if the threads are frayed.
Even if the door is only half open.

The act of remembering your roots is itself a sacred ritual.

Culture is a promise to the past. And a pathway to the future, never a performance to others.

Tiny Rituals to Begin Again

Ritual doesn't have to be dramatic. It doesn't require incense or ancient chants (though you're welcome to bring those, too). Sometimes, ritual is just permission; a quiet moment that says: *I'm still here. I'm still trying.* And that counts for something.

In a world obsessed with constant novelty, ritual is quiet rebellion. It's choosing repetition over reinvention. Meaning over metrics. Presence over performance. A moment, some calm in the storm.

Tiny rituals might save your morning. Your mind. Your messy day. Your sense of self.

Try these:

- Lighting a candle before you start your day. A small symbol that work is beginning, and that you are more than your to-do list.

- Washing your hands slowly when the day feels chaotic; imagining the stress leaving your fingers and slipping down the drain.

- Saying thank you; not performatively, but truly before a meal, even if it's instant noodles eaten in your car.

- Leaving your phone in another room while you eat. Even just once a week.

- Putting on a particular piece of music when you're cleaning. Or when you're grieving. Or when you're trying to remember how it feels to be okay.

- Making tea the old-fashioned way; not because it's practical, but because the wait itself becomes the point.

- A Sunday Walk with no music or podcast playing.

- Writing down three things that didn't go wrong today even if one of them is just *"we got through it."*

Ritual doesn't have to be impressive. It just has to be yours.

When life frays, these rituals stitch us back together. Quietly. Gently. Without applause. And slowly, we begin again. Because the act of returning to these not habit, it's our destiny. Maybe this is our quiet power, how we can fight back against the noise.

You don't need a new version of yourself. You just need a moment; one small, consistent doorway back to you.

Let that be your ritual.

Just before dawn on the Outer Hebrides, a fisherman steps outside into the cold salt air. The sky is still ink-black, the sea a sleeping thing. Before he unties the boat, before a single net is cast, he kneels.

He places one hand on the wooden hull, the other over his heart, and whispers the names of his father and grandfather. He doesn't know if he believes in God, not in the way books describe. But he believes in tides. In ancestors. In generations of men who earnt from the sea. In the rhythm of return.

He takes a small stone from his coat pocket; not for luck, but for memory and places it at the bow. Just for a moment. Just long enough to say: I am not alone out here.

No one sees him. No one claps. It is not content.

It is continuity.

The Quiet Ones Aren't Broken

You pass them in the supermarket.

Maybe they're young. Maybe they're old. They step aside, say "sorry" even when they've done nothing wrong; as if their very presence is an inconvenience.

They dip their head slightly, reluctant to meet your gaze. Odd socks maybe. An ill-fitting shirt. A softness in the way they move through the world.

You catch the bus. They're there too, sitting quietly, staring at their feet, stealing glances at the clouds outside the window. Trying not to take up space.

Our world is full of these people. The quiet ones.

And too often, the world mistakes them for weak. As if silence means uncertainty. As if not juggling like the jesters of old to the beat of standardisation means not mattering.

But here's the truth: they are carrying more than most ever see. They hear things others don't; the hush in the trees, the tension in a room, the story behind someone's sigh. They listen deeply. Think carefully. They don't speak just to fill the air.

When they do speak, they choose their words like seeds. Planted with care. Given meaning.

They are not broken. They're just holding the threads others overlook, the quiet ones that still matter.

And if you're one of them, I want you to know: I see you. You are cherished. You are loved. I don't mistake your silence for weakness. I know you're paying attention.

Maybe somewhere along the way, you made a quiet choice: Why speak, if no one will listen? Why stand out, if no one wants to see?

But hear this: We see you. I see you.

I've written stories about people like you, because your strength moves me. Because you remind me that stillness is not absence. Its power held gently. Lived honestly.

And in a world that often forgets the quiet ones, you are a reminder that gentleness is still a form of resistance. And a kind one is never truly alone.

You were never invisible to the ones who see with care.

Before We Go on *Part II goes deeper. So, here's something a bit lighter. Self-help, of the kind that still feels human.*

Self-Help for the Kind Ones: 30 Quiet Acts of Survival

1. Drink water like it's a tiny act of rebellion.
   You're not a machine. You're a camel with a long desert trek ahead.

2. Let the dishes sit. Just for now. Let stillness win this round.
   But don't let them grow new life forms

3. Forgive yourself for forgetting what day it is.

4. Name the plants on your windowsill. Or the cobwebs in the corner. Make them part of your story.
   Just don't name them Huglesias, people will judge you

5. Put on socks that don't match. Declare it fashion. Or protest. Or poetry.

6. Cancel one thing. Just one. Let that be enough.
   Just not your electricity bill. Let's stay realistic.

7. Put your phone in another room. Let it miss you for once.

8. Write a letter to your 12-year-old self. Try not to give advice. *They wouldn't listen anyway.*

9. Eat something that doesn't come with guilt. Or packaging. Or a productivity quote on the label.
   This doesn't mean a mukbang from 10 fast food restaurants

10. Some days your face forgets how to smile. That's okay. Let it rest.

11. Take three deep breaths, but do them dramatically. Like you're in a slow-motion scene in a film no one made.
    But don't hyperventilate

12. Buy one single plant. Give it a backstory. Pretend it's judging you.

13. Look at the clouds. Find the patterns and shapes, let your imagination roam.

14. Play music that makes your chest ache like a memory. Let it undo you, gently.
    If it's the Vengaboys... no judgment. Just mild concern.

15. Say no. Just... no. No reason. No footnote.

16. Put your hand on your own chest and say: "We're still here."
    That's the miracle.

17. Let someone else be loud today. You don't have to compete. You never did.

18. Draw something badly. Frame it anyway.
    Congratulations, you're officially postmodern.

19. Open a window. Let the world know you're still breathing.
    Germans have this cool word: Stoßlüften opening all the windows for a few minutes, even in winter. Try it.

20. Hold someone in your heart for a moment longer than usual. That counts. They will feel it.

21. Take a break before you earn it. Rest is not a reward.

22. Wrap yourself in a blanket like its chainmail for the soft-hearted.
    Just… not actual chainmail.

23. Stand in the sun for two minutes. Just stand. Let the photons do their work.
    Except if you're in Australia, because let's face it, the sun's a little too close down here.

24. Speak out loud when alone. It can be amazingly cathartic.
    Just don't swear at yourself too loudly. The neighbours already have 000 on speed dial.

25. Look out the window. Pretend you are in a music video.
    Main character energy restored.

26. Touch something real: wood, water, dirt, paper. Let texture interrupt the algorithm.

27. Applaud yourself. Silently. Or with jazz hands.

28. Read the kindest sentence in a book you love. Read it again. Whisper it this time. Picture it.
    Comics count. Especially the good ones.

29. Do one thing slower than usual. A spoonful. A sentence. A stare. Linger in the shower. Five more minutes won't break the world.

30. Forgive yourself for not knowing what to do next. Then turn the page anyway.

Part II
The Hollowing: What We Lost While We Optimised

The Day Your Job Became Your Identity

It happened so gradually you didn't notice at first.

At a party, someone asked, "So what do you do?" and for the first time, you didn't mention what you loved. You named your role. Your title. Your company. And they nodded like they understood something about you. And you let them.

And that was the shift.

That moment; small, polite, forgettable, became the template and marked your transition to adulthood.

You became your job. Your work became your worth. Worse than that, you became the assumptions others made about your job, based only on its title. The metrics of your output replaced the map of your interior life. The person you were at rest, in joy, in love; they quietly moved to the margins.

It's not that you stopped being yourself. It's just that there was less and less room for that self to stretch.

The things you once did for joy, sketching, wandering, dreaming, singing. These now needed to be productive. Or promotable. Or, at the very least, post-worthy.

The pressure was subtle but constant. You were taught to "brand" yourself. Told to "network" instead of make friends. Encouraged to "monetise your passions" until even your joy became a business opportunity. And anything that didn't offer returns; emotional, social, or financial, was quietly abandoned.

You weren't asked what moved you. Only what you could sell.

It didn't start with you. The seeds were sown long ago, in the factories of the Industrial Revolution, where people were first measured by their output per hour, not their character. The transformation deepened in the 20th century, but it was the 1970s with the rise of corporate culture, self-help for profit, and neoliberal individualism that saw work begin to replace identity.

Careers weren't just how you survived; they became who you were.

We forgot how to introduce ourselves without the armour of a role. We forgot how to answer, "Who are you?" without listing what we do. And slowly, the person beneath the title began to fade like a background character in their own life.

But it wasn't always this way. In some cultures, and communities, your introduction wasn't your occupation. It was your village, your family, your story. You were known not by what you achieved, but by who you belonged to. The welder's laugh, the mechanics patience, the midwife's gentleness; these were identities built on presence, not productivity. They didn't vanish with a job loss or career shift. They endured.

You can return to the self that existed before the LinkedIn bio. The self that danced badly in kitchens. That lost time in books. That laughed until they couldn't breathe, not because it was useful, but because it was real.

You are more than your job title. You always were.

The Performance of Professionalism

Somewhere along the way, being "professional" stopped meaning reliable or respectful. Now it has the meaning silent, sterile, and separate from yourself.

We learned to speak in careful scripts. To keep our faces neutral. To hide our accents, our grief, our joy. To smile at injustice, nod through discomfort, and turn our volume down just enough to fit in.

Professionalism became a costume. A tone of voice. A set of plain colours and acceptable feelings. We wore ties and white shirts as symbols of submission. For years wore it so well that we forgot we had ever been anything else.

But the cost was quiet erasure of the self.

Because under the banner of being "professional," we learned not to cry. Not to challenge. Not to bring our whole selves to the room. We learned that passion was too much, softness was weakness, and that showing care made us suspect, irrational, needing retraining.

Women were told they were too emotional. People of colour were told they were too loud, too angry, too much. Neurodivergent people were told they needed to mask. We were all told adapt, or be seen as unfit for the workplace.

Structures arose to support the corporate entities. Too distraught? We have workplace counselling for that. Too irrational? We can performance manage you for that. Too distracted? Here's a timetable to fix you.

There is a reason why tv shows like Severance hit so hard. Because they don't just show a possible future; they show a present we're already living in.

What good are we to anyone if we're not allowed to be fully alive in what we do?
But no need to worry; those roles are going to AI now.
Emotions were always inconvenient. Chatbots don't cry.

You are not unprofessional for being a human.
You are not weak for needing a moment.
You are not wrong for asking why things feel so off.

Maybe what they call unprofessional is often just someone remembering who they are; a quiet attempt by one soul to break free from the shackles of conformity and become, once again, what our ancestors intended.

And maybe the strongest thing you can do isn't to perform to their tune but to model humanity.

The Grief of the Nonlinear Life

A parent reheats coffee for the third time. A freelancer stares at their open tabs, each one a different hustle; none of them a home. A carer glances at the clock, not to be on time for a meeting, but for medication. None of it fits on a business card. But all of it is work. All of it is worth.

We were told life was a line. School, job, promotion, retirement; as if humanity were a conveyor belt. But real lives meander. They pause. They double back. They care for sick parents, raise children, burn out, heal, reinvent. And yet, we grieve our divergence from the script, as if our detours are failures rather than richness.

Especially for women, stepping out to raise children is still framed as opting out, not contributing. As if nurturing life is somehow less meaningful than attending meetings. When women return? They're expected to act like nothing changed, while everything did. Even now, many hide the gaps in their resumes like bruises instead of the badges of love and labour they truly are. This, while societies complain about falling birth rates and wonder why. When they have made having a child as impracticable and unsupported as possible.

Not all paths are vertical. The best stories you ever read in fiction are not the most predictable ones. Paths in life stretch sideways, into stories that no resume' can capture. There is grief, yes. Grief for the recognition not given, for the milestones not met. But there is also grace. You get to be the author of a life not measured by ladders, but by depth.

Your value was never linear.

Neither is your life.

And maybe that's the invitation.

To stop measuring life in job titles, promotions, or neatly filled timelines and start noticing the deeper things.
The way you make someone feel heard on their worst day.
The lessons you learned when life didn't go to plan.
The strength it takes to slow down when everything tells you to speed up.

Your life doesn't need to follow the chart.
It doesn't need to impress anyone. It just needs to belong to you

The Age of Constant Comparison

The Scroll

She tells herself she's tired.
She's showered, the bathroom light is still warm.
Beside her in bed, her partner breathes deep.
He is steady, safe. Her ship in the storm.
She loves him. He adores her.
There's no tension. No unspoken words.

And yet.

She reaches for the phone.
Just for a moment.

Thirty-seven minutes later, she's in Positano. Or maybe Santorini.
A friend-of-a-friend's wedding, all bright dresses and laughter
with a golden sunset. The bride glows. The guests look
effortlessly free. A child tosses flower petals into the breeze.

She looks at her own arm, resting on a creased bedsheet,
wrapped in yesterday's pyjamas and feels a flicker of something
she can't quite name.

Her day was fine. Rewarding, even.
A smile from a stranger.
A walk beneath winter trees.
Pasta cooked just right.
The smile of her lover.

But now it all feels smaller. Dimmed by contrast.

She glances at her partner again, asleep. The one who knows her laugh, who kisses her temple when she's anxious, who brought her tea this morning without needing a reason.

She knows she should put the phone down.
Reach out. Touch his skin.
Let the realness of him guide her to sleep.

But instead, her hand scrolls on.

Because somewhere in that glowing square of glass, the world seems shinier. Tidier. Edited.

And still, she scrolls.
Chasing something the screen will never give back.

When the Mirror Was Local

There was a time not long ago, when the people we compared ourselves to were the ones we knew. Like really knew.

The kid down the road who made the football team.
The neighbour with perfect garden.
The cousin who got a better grade in maths.

That was the scale. That was the village.

Comparison was bounded. Contextual.
You envied the new car, but you also saw the arguments in that driveway.
You admired her job, but you also knew her dad was sick, and she spent her weekends supporting him.

Proximity made people real.
Their wins were visible. but so were their cracks. You could still ache with jealousy, but that ache lived beside empathy and awareness. That made a difference.

Now, the mirror has shattered and scattered.

You compare your Tuesday afternoon to someone's honeymoon in Bali. Your living room to an influencer's fifth renovation. Your body to someone who's paid to maintain theirs like it's a full-time job; because it is.

And the worst part? These comparisons are endless.
Global. Curated. There is no limit anymore to ones suffering if your mind wants to feel jealousy.

You used to look across the street.
Now you're measuring yourself against a billion edited strangers and wondering why you feel so behind.

Please know you're not behind. You're just human and the scale is broken.
Those people you see? Many of them are also sitting there, on their phones, comparing themselves to others, and not feeling adequate either.
Our souls weren't built to carry the weight of the world's applause, or its judgment.
We were made for glances.
For village-sized mirrors.
For being seen by a few, not consumed by all.

The Illusion of Effortless Lives

We know it's curated. We *know*.
And still, it gets to us.

The woman with the serene yoga pose on a cliff at sunrise? She's out of frame ten minutes later, arguing with her partner over which angle or filter looks 'most authentic'.
The laughing dad doing the viral family video? They rehearsed it twelve times. The kids are tired. He's tired. But the edit goes live and we believe it. We don't mean to. But we do.

Because algorithms reward the polished. The dramatic. The beautiful. What we see most becomes what we expect; not just of others, but of ourselves.

And that's the trap.

You start to feel like you're the only one whose moments are… unfinished. Whose mornings are messy. You wonder if everyone else is living with more ease, more grace, more glow.

But real life was never meant to be a 30-second clip. It was never meant to be clipped at all.

Think of the great authors, the ones who spent entire pages describing a room, or a slow walk through the mist. A kettle warming. A lamplighter moving through the village square at night in a remote part of Borneo. A silence that stretched like ribbon between two people in love.

Moments used to be allowed to unfold and they were rich, layered, slow.

Now, moments must land. They must impress. They must fit within a square, and finish before the swipe.

And so, we rush our own lives. We start trimming the edges of our joy so it'll feel more shareable.

But nothing truly sacred fits neatly into a clip.
The best parts of life aren't highlight reels. They're blurry, unfiltered, and often not seen at all.

When Dreams Became Products

Once, a dream was something personal.
You wanted to write a book. Run a café. Help rescue stray animals. Dance until your legs gave out. It was yours, and maybe a few close people knew.

Now? Dreams are content.

Your goals are expected to be brandable. Optimised. Public. Tracked with a printable planner from Etsy and your progress listed for others to see.

Even healing, something once so tender and private has been rebranded as lifestyle.
"Glow-up culture." "Soft life." Aesthetics of rest and recovery, polished until they're post-worthy. And beneath the glow? Burnout. Comparison. Quiet shame that you're not evolving fast

enough. There's always a link to buy. A course to join. A product to add to your cart.

It's no longer enough to live your life, you are expected to monetise it. Your body becomes a brand. Your thoughts, a thread. Your routine, a reel.

Whole platforms have developed out this, entire industries.

Even childhood is shifting. Ask kids what they want to be when they grow up, and more than ever, they'll say "influencer."
Not teacher. Not pilot. Influencer, as if the highest good is to be watched and commodified.

We have blurred the line between the personal and the public. And in doing so, we've lost something sacred: the right to grow quietly. To fail privately. To change our minds without making a post about it.

Some parents now find themselves torn between their desire for privacy and the lure of performance. The result?
Oversized emojis covering their children's faces in family photos. Seriously? Just set your account to private, or maybe don't post at all.

Not everything has to be seen.
Not everything has to scale.
There is meaning in living a life that isn't designed for display where strangers can't learn your habits, heartbreaks, or daily rituals from a single search.

The Scrolling Never Ends

Books have a final page. Films have credits.

Even conversations eventually end; someone yawns, or the tea goes cold.

But the feed? The feed never stops.

There's no natural pause, no moment of closure. Just more. Another clip. Another quote. Another polished day-in-the-life.

You tell yourself: *Just one more scroll.* And forty-five minutes later, you're somewhere between a skincare tutorial, a breakup confession, and memorising a stranger's pantry.

You are full, but not nourished. Stimulated, but not satisfied.

That's by design. The infinite scroll was engineered to keep you reaching. It mimics gambling, not reading. There's no rhythm of beginning, middle, and end, just an endless loop of dopamine flickers.

Our brains were never meant to live in that loop.
They need endings. They need stillness. They need the grace of enough.

But with the feed, there is no "enough." You never see the words: "You're full now. Go outside. Touch a tree. Call a friend. Make soup."

Instead, it leaves you suspended in a kind of low-grade longing. Like you're always almost there; if you just scroll a little further, click one more link, improve one more habit.

But you never arrive. Because the goalpost isn't real. And the "there" was always just... here.

We're All Behind Together

As we touched on, people posting the shiny moments? They feel behind, too.

That woman in Santorini, she's scrolling someone else's feed. The dad with the perfect family picnic? He's wondering if he's doing enough. Even the wellness coach with the colour-coded fridge planner and morning affirmations? She has days where she feels like she's falling apart, and her wellness business is failing.

Behind the curtain so many are struggling. Because everyone is chasing the same idea. Monetise yourself. Stream. Promote. Perform. Supply now far exceeds demand in this vicious circus.

The apps don't care how you feel; only that you keep reaching. The standard keeps shifting and the goals keep moving. And we keep chasing. Faster, harder, shinier.

But the strange and comforting truth is: Almost everyone feels behind. Almost everyone is measuring themselves against something that doesn't really exist.

You are not the only one.

We are all on this strange carousel, spinning faster than it was ever meant to go. Gripping our phones with quiet fear, hoping to feel something, hoping to feel enough.

So, if you're reading this and nodding… you're not alone. If your chest sometimes tightens after an hour of staring at the screen… you're not alone. If you've ever cried after a perfectly good day because someone else's highlight made yours feel small… You are absolutely, deeply, not alone.

And maybe the way off the carousel starts here; not with a perfect solution, but with a shared exhale.

We're in the same boat. Not behind. Not broken. Just here, trying, feeling, human.

Reclaiming Enough

You are not behind. You are not missing out. You are not doing life wrong. You are living. You are here. And the truth is that was always enough.

Not every part of your life has to mean something to someone else.
Your morning coffee, in the same chipped mug whilst you look out at the dew on the morning grass.
Your child resting their head on your shoulder without a word whilst you finish your favourite book.

These are not small things. They are everything.

The world will keep spinning fast. The feed will keep humming. But you don't have to keep up.

Maybe you step outside tonight look at those stars (or even streetlights!). Feel the cool air. Let it remind you you're still alive. Put the phone down. Touch someone's hand. Remember what real skin feels like; warm, imperfect, living. You are not a brand. You are not a product. And we need to stop feeding the beast.

You're a person. A whole, unfolding, messy miracle of one.

And somewhere, quietly, that is more than enough.

The Myth of Emotional Capitalism

You were told to share your story.

They said it would be freeing, that vulnerability was strength. Everyone was doing it. You even liked watching content like that. It felt raw, connected, unbridled.
As if the emotion came through the screen and you were... there. And you wanted to be a part of that, just on the other side of the lens.

You thought that if you just opened up, others would understand you. Connect with you. Feel your pain. And maybe be there for you.

And for a moment, they did. Some watched, you saw it on the view count. But then came the silence after the post. The likes that didn't come, the feeling that maybe you didn't cry the right way. That maybe the words sounded a bit selfish. You started to wonder if you didn't embellish it enough to get them to connect with you.

Your hair was a bit messy. The camera was out of focus for a moment. Was the video too long? Perhaps a short would have been better.

But what is wrong with these people?
They watched me cry, I know they did.
But they didn't like it, are they trying to hurt me?
Maybe I should buy a better camera filter.
Change the lip gloss, delete it and try again.
Does no one care? I told them my secrets.

You were told that sharing would set you free. But no one told you it might also put you on display. That somewhere along the way, storytelling became a marketing strategy. Pain became content. Healing became a performance.

You are not alone in this.

Thousands feel it: that ache when a post meant to express turns into a desire for it to succeed.

The distortion creeps in slowly of course. You begin editing your grief. Rehearsing your authenticity. And all of it feels… wrong. But the algorithm doesn't reward quiet honesty. It rewards spectacle.

Somewhere in the mess of shares, filters, and metrics, your pain was no longer yours. It became a product that was packaged and performative. There is a name for this: emotional capitalism. And it thrives on convincing you that your truth only matters if it trends.

The cruel irony? It told us to share more, feel more, show more. But only in the right way with the right lighting. The right voice, the right length to get views. It promised connection, and delivered exposure.

And now, left wondering what it means to be real at all.

The False Promise

In 2021, the *Journal of American College Health* defined the term **Sadfishing**; when social media users exaggerate their emotional state online to gain sympathy.

That was four years ago. What was once a "shocking trend" is now standard practice, where people feel compelled to not only expose their emotional vulnerability online for the world to see, but to *amplify* it, shape it, perform it.

And before we judge the exaggeration, let's remember: They're just trying to survive the feed. Just trying to stay visible in a world where algorithms punish quiet pain.

Because in the world of clicks, if no one clicks, does anyone really care?

The problem with emotional vulnerability in front of a camera is that the line between truth and performance blurs, even to the person sharing it. You begin to edit your pain, rehearse your breakdowns. Choose which version of your grief gets the most engagement.

This is why someone truly falling apart might receive silence or cruelty, while someone acting out a curated breakdown, framed just right, receives love and applause.

The world says it wants authenticity. But only to a point. It wants honesty, but only from people attractive enough, composed enough, on-brand enough to deliver it in a palatable frame.

When this becomes normal, when even our vulnerability must be stylized to survive, the expectation seeps into every corner of our lives. Into peer groups and friendships. Into moments that should've been sacred.

And if you *did* share it…Was it still yours? Is anything yours really after its posted to the world?

Quiet Resistance

I want you to think about the last time you were truly emotional. Not just sad, but gutted, unfiltered, lost. Tears you didn't plan, rage and sobbing you didn't choreograph.

Chances are, there wasn't a camera in sight. You weren't performing, you weren't even processing. You were just feeling. Fully.

Because we are not meant to emote on cue like seasoned actors. We're meant to respond to life around us, not the blinking light of a record button.

Some of the most real moments you'll ever live through… will be seen only by your dog. Your goldfish. Or your one weird friend who puts up with you regardless. And that's okay.

Not everything needs to be an audience event and not every wound needs to be wrapped in commentary.

Let it be private, let it be yours. Let the clout chasers chase and let the false families rehearse their skits. Let others monetise their grief if they choose.

But your soul is sacred.
And sacred things are not content.

A Note of Grace

We don't judge. I certainly don't.

I have days where I feel lower than low, where I scroll through emotional content chasing that little drop of dopamine. Sometimes it's comforting to see others feel deeply. It makes us feel less alone.

Because the world can be cruel and we all need a sugary treat now and then.

But you are not a product. You are not here to be commodified, compared, or measured by how "authentic" your pain looks through a camera lens.

Your story doesn't need a filter to be real. Your heart doesn't need a caption to be felt. You don't need to be seen by strangers to be valid.

In a world of performers, we need to be a poet. And if the world doesn't clap?

Good.

You weren't performing for it anyway.

Human Dignity Vs Market Logic

In the last part, we explored how our emotions are our own, how they don't need to be monetised or performed to be real, how we can be private and lead a more fulfilling life because of it.

Now, we widen the lens. Because it's not just our feelings that are commodified, it's us as people. In this chapter, we ask something harder:

What does the world see when it looks at you? A person? Or a productivity metric?

Put simply, we're exploring how society often defines our value in economic terms. I know, big words. That's okay. Big words are how we know we're not just scrolling TikTok, right?

Let's slow it down with a scene.

Have you ever been to the shops and noticed that one person in line, the one who takes *forever*?

Maybe they're elderly, or just confused. Maybe they're paying with a pocketful of change, digging into a well-loved purse, whispering to the cashier with a kind of nervous apology in their voice. Maybe they're just moving at a different rhythm than the rest of us.

You've seen them. You've *been* behind them.

And maybe if we're being honest, you got frustrated. You felt that itch. That impulse to sigh, to tap your foot, to glance at your phone, to *feel the weight of time* pressing against your chest.

Not because you had anywhere to be, not really. But because… something in you whispered, *they're too slow for the system.* Whatever that system is.

In that moment, we don't value them, we value speed and value efficiency. We value frictionless transactions and uninterrupted flow.

But what if instead of seeing an inconvenience we saw an invitation? A small window to breathe, to look around the store, to notice the quiet stories playing out around us? What if that moment in line became a chance to soften, not harden?

Most of the time, we don't see the invitation, we just move on irritated if not outright dismissive.

Because here's the quiet truth: The logic of the market doesn't care about grace. It doesn't care if someone's having a hard day. It doesn't care if someone is lonely, or slow, or new to the process. It cares about performance, speed, scalability.

You see it in the chirp of self-checkouts; machines that never say "thank you," never reward your patience, never even notice the kind thing you just did.

You stopped in that self-checkout for a moment to help someone find their card? The machine says: *Unexpected item in the bagging area*. No applause. No recognition. Just error codes and blinking lights.

This is the quiet war we all face now. And I assure you we are all in the trenches together.:

Market logic rewards speed but dignity lives in slowness.

It lives in patience and eye contact. It lives in those small invisible acts, the ones no performance review or marketing agency can track. But damn, they would if they could.

The Last Kind Ones feel this tension deeply. You feel it in workplaces where numbers matter more than people. You feel it in conversations where efficiency has replaced curiosity. You feel it in job interviews that treat you like a resource, not a person. That's even if you are lucky enough to speak to a person at all, and not get filtered by an AI that glitches out half way through, resulting in an automatic rejection of you.

And yet, even in this system, some still choose kindness over competition.

We see this most clearly in roles like caregiving, aged care, disability support; roles filled by people drawn not to profit, but to purpose. People who don't calculate the worth of their time in dollars per hour, but in connection per moment.

And what does the market give them in return?

Low pay, burnout, contracts that treat compassion like a liability. Because the market doesn't know how to price love. So, it pretends it's worth less.

These are the souls who show up because their heart *knows*. And still society pays them only what it must. Because kindness, it seems, isn't billable.

But even beyond the workplace we see small refusals everywhere. Small candles in the darkness that tell us not all is lost if we keep fighting against it.

The person who steps aside and helps the elderly man at the pharmacy instead of rushing past. The teen who stops to walk someone across the road, even if their friends scoff. The stranger who holds the door just a little longer, even when no one's looking.

These are acts that don't increase GDP. They don't get added to quarterly reports, but they matter more.

They are how dignity survives, how being human quietly resists being reduced to usefulness, algorithms, data.

So, remember this, especially when the world tries to shrink you down into a number, a stat, a "value add":

Being valuable to the market is not the same as being valuable to humanity.

You can drive a Mercedes; yes, that's market value. You can ride a pushbike and care for your grandfather, that's *human value*.

They're not mutually exclusive. But let's be honest we all know which one matters more when the noise dies down.

Let the world chase performance, let it chase speed. But hold onto your softness and your patience. Your small acts that go don't unnoticed.

Because in the end?

Human dignity isn't inefficient. It's what keeps the world bearable. And if we are going to get back to that more, we need to keep fighting by these small actions. Resistance has never been more beautiful and human.

What Can't Be Automated (Yet)

A soft manifesto for the sacred, the soulful, and the stubbornly human; the things that resist optimisation, even now.

There's a reason people still long for presence.
Even in a world where AI can respond with sympathy,
no machine truly grieves with you at a funeral.
No app holds your hand while you cry.
No shortcut carries the weight of a body sitting beside you when words fail. Some things still resist automation.

In a world that optimises everything including clicks, calories, emotions, productivity, personality; it's easy to forget that not all value is quantifiable. That not every sacred thing can be made efficient. The best parts of being alive are often wildly inefficient by design.

The Algorithm Can't Tuck You In

You can buy a smart blanket that heats itself.
You can schedule a white noise machine to fade out as you drift off.
But nothing can replace the small ritual of someone saying, "Goodnight. I'm right here."

We forget how much of life is built on gestures like that, not for their practicality, but for their presence. The cup of tea made for no reason.
The dog's tail thumping against the floor just because you walked in. The letter written in longhand, even though it could've been a text.

These are the slow, unautomated things. The kind that doesn't have an algorithm. But they are the anchors of humanity.

The Soul Refuses to Be Streamlined

There is no spreadsheet that can show you what you meant to your grandmother. No metric to explain the soft ache of missing someone before they're gone. No KPI to measure the joy of watching a toddler try to say *"spaghetti."*

Your soul will not become a product line; it will resist and bloom in the places the screen doesn't see.

We are not here to outperform, trying is a fool's errand. We are here to outlove, outcare, outlisten. Outlast the noise.

What's Left When Everything Else Is Machine

The machines now write better essays, draw better faces, even hold better conversations. But they will never connect with your silence the way a friend can. They will never *mean it* when they ask how you are. They will never ache to hold someone who hurts.

So here is what can't be automated (yet):

- The pause after a joke, where two people fall into laughter and neither person wants it to end.

- Forgiveness that comes not from logic, but from love.

- The warmth of someone's hand reaching for yours in the dark.

- The quiet decision to stay when walking away would be easier.

- The shared glance across a room that says, *"I see you. I know you."*

- The way a child rests their head on your chest, trusting, unthinking, safe.

- The hug between a child and elderly parent that lingers a second too long, because it matters more than words.

- The soft rustle of trees before the wind even picks up. as if they're whispering first.

- The way flowers still bloom, without ever checking an audience is watching.

- How dusk settles over a field like a blanket; silent, slow, unquestioning.

These things are sacred. And still ours.

A Quiet Call

Don't rush to make yourself replaceable. Don't streamline your soul. Don't turn your tenderness into content.

If there's one rebellion left to us in a world of code and efficiency, it's this:

To keep doing the things that don't make sense to the algorithm, but make all the sense in the world to our hearts.

You are not a feature waiting to be updated. You are a story, a scent, a gesture, a rhythm, still human, still holy, still here.

And that's the quiet gift we carry. The world may automate our schedules, our services, even our stories but it cannot automate the sacred.

It cannot automate wonder. It cannot automate grace, and it cannot automate you.

The Last Kind Ones know this already.

We carry the torch not for the efficient but for the meaningful. We are not afraid to do things slowly, beautifully, with care.

While the world hurries on, we'll keep the soul.

The Subscription Self

There was a time when you were just you.

You didn't need a curated persona. You weren't asked to regulate your morning routine for productivity, track your sleep cycle, or explain your life in a bio. You didn't have a brand. You weren't a channel. You were a person.

But somewhere along the way, just being stopped being enough.

Now, for many of us, the self has become a service. Something you package, update, monitor, all in the hope it gets chosen. The platforms didn't ask for money at first; they asked for attention. Then content. Then consistency. Then identity.

And we gave it.

We became subscribers to our own lives.

There's an invisible pressure now, not just to be, but to appear. To show up, constantly, in all the right ways: witty but not annoying, vulnerable but not messy, smart but not threatening.
You must post, respond, engage. You must be reachable, not because you want to, but because not responding sends its own signal. Even silence has become a performance.

We live under the quiet tyranny of this. It's no longer enough to live moments, they must be captured, filtered, made shareable. A sunset isn't just for your eyes; it's for your story. Your outfit, your dinner, your Sunday morning, all gently nudged toward performance.

In this model, the self is never finished. It is a feed. A loop. And like any good service, it must always be improving.

What does that do to us?

It makes us tired in ways we don't always recognise. The kind of tired where even resting feels like failure, because you weren't producing anything.
Where you scroll not for joy, but to see what kind of person you're supposed to be today. Where you wake up with a fog of anxiety, unsure why, until you remember you haven't posted in a while, haven't replied, haven't updated.

This isn't drama. It's reality for millions. Especially for the kind ones, those who carry the double weight of being seen and staying sincere.

And the worst part? You start to believe that if you are not visible, you are not valuable.

But let's remember something softer, older, and far truer:

You are not a subscription. You are not an ongoing product. You are allowed to have off days. You are allowed to disappear, to rest, to stop performing. You are allowed to change your mind, to evolve quietly, to live a moment that no one else sees.

You are allowed to be a person.

The Last Kind Ones know this.

We know what it's like to feel trapped in the loop, and we also know there is still a way out.
Not by going off-grid and growing aubergines in the forest, dressing in bird feathers.

You are allowed to opt out. You don't need to be on every social media. You can choose ones that are better for your health, or even none at all.
Remember that beneath the feed, beneath the update, there is still a core self that needs nothing but care.

So let the metrics slip. Let the profile blur. Let the account become inactive. You were never made to be maintained; you were made to live.

And we will remind you, as many times as it takes: you do not have to earn your right to be. You already are valuable to all of us.

You are not a brand. You are not a service. You are the whole, aching, beautiful story no one else can live.

Presence for Sale

They used to call it attention.

Now they call it engagement.

But what they really mean is presence.

And somewhere along the way, your presence stopped being yours.

It started subtly, a ping, a buzz, a notification that pulled you away from the here and now. A friend tagging you in a photo. A reminder of something you forgot to want. Then came the expectation: to be reachable, to be responsive, to be performing. We were told connection online was freedom. But the terms were never ours, and let's face it, we never read the terms. We just agreed blindly.

Today, your presence is bought and sold, by apps, by platforms, by companies who care not about you, but about your dwell time online.

The average person now spends over a third of their waking hours online. That's not just a habit. That's a marketplace, and in that marketplace, the currency is you your clicks, your pauses, your attention span. Every scroll is data. Every moment you hesitate is monetized and monitored.

Presence used to mean sitting across from someone, fully listening. Feeling the world with your body (Or making sure Bob didn't steal those scrabble pieces). It's also noticing the breeze, the flicker of a candle, the sigh of someone you love. Presence meant you were there. When was the last time you stopped really, and looked up at the clouds?

Now, presence means availability. Not to people, but to platforms and to schedules. To systems that do not love you back.

We no longer ask, "Are you okay?" We ask, "Did you see my message?"

We don't say, "I've been thinking of you." We say, "Did you get my post?"

Even rest has been co-opted. Apps guide us through meditation not for healing, but for productivity. Mindfulness is marketed as performance enhancement. Sleep is a metric. Silence is a gap in market share.

What does it mean to be present in a world that monetises every moment?

It means choosing, fiercely and gently, when to reclaim your time. It means recognising the value of a quiet hour without input. It means noticing the sky. Leaving your phone behind. Letting a conversation run long. Breathing without needing to record it.

The Last Kind Ones are not Luddites. We don't reject technology. But we insist on one truth: presence must remain human.

Because when presence becomes product, the soul starts to fray.

Here's your reminder: you don't owe the world your constant availability. You don't need to be always-on. You are allowed to be where you are; fully, gently, stubbornly so.

Take your presence back.

Give it to the forest. The sea. The ones you love.

And keep a little of it just for yourself.

Not everything has to be shared.

Not everything has to be tracked.

You are not a signal. You are not a service.

You are a presence. And you are sacred.

The Last Kind Ones remember.

And we're here to remind you when you forget.

The point isn't to keep up anymore, it's to stay awake. To stay real. To become cultural relics, not because we've been left behind, but because we're caretaking something too sacred to automate. Kindness. Presence. Human grace. While the world scrambles for the next gadget, platform, or AI we need to hold the line.

The Algorithm of Belonging

We all want to belong.

That longing isn't weakness; it's a whisper from our oldest selves. The part of us that sat around fires, leaned in during storms, and scanned the horizon for someone walking back home. It's older than language. And in that ancient longing lies our most human vulnerability.

But today, belonging is no longer found around fires. It's found in feeds. Or so we are told.

The modern web promises us tribes, communities, kindred spirits. It whispers that if we just post enough, engage enough, share the right things at the right time, we will be welcomed. Not just seen, but celebrated. The lonely will be less lonely. The soft will be safe.

And for a time, maybe that felt true. But what happens when algorithms shape our sense of belonging, when they change who we are at the core?

Algorithms reward repetition and amplify the loudest. They sort us into silos, they punish nuance. And slowly, without noticing, we start having not connection, but compliance. We post not what we feel, but what performs well. Not what matters, but what pleases. Belonging becomes conditional, the need to perform correctly, and you can stay.

We begin to split. Into who we are, and who is most likely to be liked. And that gap? It's where the ache begins.

For the Last Kind Ones, this is especially sharp. We are drawn to truth, to softness, to the grey areas that don't go viral.

We long for connection, but not at the cost of authenticity, as we know the difference. So, we fall quiet, not because we don't care, but because we do.

And in this quiet, we begin to wonder: what if we don't fit the algorithm? What if our belonging can't be engineered?

Here's what we must remember:

Belonging isn't earned by pleasing strangers online. It's felt in the places where silence is allowed, where no performance is required. Where your laugh is welcome even if it arrives at the wrong moment. Where your story doesn't need a headline.

The algorithm will always move faster than the soul. It optimises for stickiness, not for sanctity. For engagement, not for empathy.

Then we step back. We whisper instead of shout. We must write instead of react. We must gather instead of follow We must remember that the ones who matter are not metrics. And in that remembering, we begin to find each other again.

You do not need to earn your belonging. You already belong.

The Last Kind Ones are waiting. We always were.

When Work Became Content

There was a time when work ended.

You clocked out, stepped away, went home. The work stayed behind; on the factory floor, in the office tray, behind the counter. You might carry the weight of it in your body or heart, but the world allowed you, at least in name, to stop.

Now, work follows us. It has shapeshifted. It no longer lives in places with defined boundaries; it lives in us. And more dangerously, it lives in our feeds.

Today, work is content. The teacher must perform their teaching. The builder must film each brick they lay. The artist must explain their process, their vision, their pain. And the human? They must prove they are worth watching.

This is not documentation. It is demand. Perform, or disappear. Share, or be forgotten. Promotion is now essential; not to get ahead even, just to maintain. Even leisure is now opportunity: a hike is content, a moment of peace is a potential Reel, a kind gesture becomes marketable.

It is no longer enough to do the work; you must package it, prettify it, publish it.

And behind every post that whispers "Here's what I made"
 is a silent question: "Was it enough to matter?"

The erosion is slow, but it is real. Not all labor is visible. Not all value is scalable. Not all meaning is marketable; but in a system that only measures the seen, the show becomes the standard.

The Last Kind Ones know this tension well. Many of us are tired, not from the making, but from the proving. From feeling like our efforts don't count unless someone claps. But we do not need applause to affirm our dignity.

Some of the most important work is never uploaded. Some of the most honest living leaves no trace.

Here's what we say:

- You can write something beautiful and never post it.

- You can care deeply for someone and not film it.

- You can rest without turning it into a productivity hack.

- You can build quietly. And still be worthy.

Work is sacred when it serves, when it heals, when it builds. It does not need to be consumed to be real.

Let your work be enough, even when unseen. Let your rest be enough, even when unshared. Let your worth be enough, even when unmeasured.

The Last Kind Ones are not chasing virality. We are building something that lasts. And not everything that lasts makes noise.

The Last Meaningful Gesture

There is a moment that's small, quiet, unnoticed, when a person, despite everything, chooses kindness.
It might be as simple as letting someone go ahead in a queue. Or washing the dishes without being asked. Or checking in on someone who hasn't been themselves.
It's not content. It's just... good.

In a world that rewards performance, these acts make little sense. They offer no return on investment, no audience, no applause. They are, by all economic logic, inefficient.

And yet they are what is left when the noise fades, they are what remains in the photo albums of old and the memories of yesterday.

The Last Kind Ones understand this. Because we've done it. Again and again.
Sometimes without even knowing why, only that it felt right at the moment. That to walk past would cost us something deeper than time.

These gestures matter not because they are large, but because they resist a world that wants everything to be calculated. They are the acts that whisper, *"I am still human. And so are you"*.

In a time when the world feels cold, the last meaningful gesture is a quiet defiance.
A candle in the algorithmic dark.

Maybe no one sees it.
Maybe no one thanks you.

But you did it anyway.

And in doing so, you reminded the world gently, stubbornly, that care is not a transaction.

Somewhere, someone felt it. Maybe not in words. Maybe not right away.

But it reached them.

If you've ever:

- Helped someone cross the street without filming it.

- Wrote a letter you never sent.

- Took a call at midnight because someone needed to talk.

- Let someone cry without rushing to fix it.

Then you've made the gesture. And you should know, it mattered.

We're nearing the end of this part of the book, but not the end of each other.
Every small act builds the bridge.
Every quiet choice adds to what comes next.

The world may not remember every click or scroll.

But it remembers the last meaningful gesture.

And so do we.

The Last Kind Ones are not here to be famous.
We're here to be felt.
To make something worth remembering.
Even if it's only by one person.
Even if it's only once.

That's enough.

Part III
The Return: What We Remembered

There comes a point in every journey where the road stops winding away and begins to lead home again; not to the world as it was, but to what we carry from it.

This final section is about resisting the world as it is, and remembering who we are beneath it all. After the burnout, after the loneliness of endless performance we collectively return. Not with slogans or sleek solutions, but with slowness. With a bowl of warm soup, a hand on a shoulder, a truth we don't need to explain.

These chapters are a kind of firelight; a place to gather, to breathe, to remember. Not because we've escaped the system, but because we've remembered: we are not it. And somewhere out there, quietly but certainly, others are remembering too.

The world will not keep spinning in this direction forever. A turning is coming. A reckoning, a great remembering if you will. And if we stay awake until then, if we stay kind, and stubborn, and human, we can help bring that future into being.

We are not here to accelerate.

We are here to tend the soil and grow something useful for the future. Together.

·

Refusing the Performance

The lights are always on now. The curtain never falls.

We live inside an endless stage, our roles stretching across timelines, platforms, messages, and feeds. Even when we don't mean to, we act. We curate. We pose. Not always out of vanity but out of habit and survival. Out of a fundamental need for connection in a world that can feel so alone.

Yet something in us remembers how to leave the theatre. Even when it's hard to see the door from the stage.

The Last Kind Ones are those who feel this tension; with weariness. We are tired of performing versions of ourselves for approval. Tired of treating life like a setlist. We are often misunderstood for our quietness, or for moments when we were awkward, or too emotional.

So, we've begun stepping away. Quietly. Bravely. We exit stage left.

Why?

Because we've seen through the fog. We've lifted the veil of social media and modern-day mediocrity. And with a trembling hand, we've seen the world for what it is, and felt its pain in full.

But we don't dwell in the despair. We begin again. Brick by brick, gesture by gesture.

There is a woman in Kyoto who sweeps the temple steps before sunrise. Not for the tourists who will come, but out of respect for ancestor's past. She hums, though no one hears. The brush against stone is her rhythm. She finishes with a small bow to the morning.

There is a man in rural Wales who drinks his tea while fog folds over the hills. His sheep are still sleeping. The only sound is the kettle cooling on the stove. He doesn't post a photo. He simply watches.

To refuse the performance of the modern stage is not to disappear, go off-grid, grow a beard, and speak only to an iguana named Trevor. It is to live without applause. To act without witness. To feel joy without proof.

It's the opposite of the IKEA aesthetic and warmer than flatpack furniture could ever be.

The world will tell you this is failure. But the soul knows it as peace with every brush of morning breeze against your skin.

We need a return to the self behind the mask. The self that does not ask "Was it good enough?" but simply breathes, "I am here."

Because sometimes, the bravest thing you can do is not share it.
You can bake a cake and not take a photo.
You can give a gift and never mention it.
You can dance alone with no audience but the dust in the light.

The Last Kind Ones are not vanishing.

We are remembering.

And when the performance ends, when the curtain falls there is still a life.

And it is ours.

Stillness in a Monetised World

Stillness is not easy to find these days.

Not because there is nowhere quiet, but because the world has taught us to fear it. To sit still is to fall behind. To pause is to become invisible. To rest is to be left out. We live in a culture where every moment is an opportunity, or a missed one. Even silence has become a space to optimise.

Stillness is the embodiment of everything we have forgotten to cherish.

There is a young man in Kerala who walks barefoot through the morning mist. He works at a call centre by night, but these early hours belong to him.
He does not post his walk. He simply walks. Through spice-scented air and dew-laced leaves, passing the jasmine flower sellers who are getting set up for the day, he is alone with his thoughts and the birds.

There is a woman in Alaska who spends her evenings knitting beside a wood stove.
 Her phone is powered off. Outside, snow presses gently against the windows with a light howl of the night air pressing against the panes. Inside, the soft click of needles and crackle off the wood burning is the only sound. Her stillness is not shared. But it fills the room. She is content.

Stillness, in a monetised world, is a quiet rebellion. A refusal to turn every breath into branding. To refuse to be monitored by your screen time and your clicks. A resistance against the pressure to constantly produce, explain, promote.

When we were young, we were taught to stop, drop and roll if there was a fire. That's how you escaped the smoke and flames presumably. Being still is the modern equivalent of that for our fast-paced world. And it's just as important for the soul as escaping the fire was meant to be as a child.

You are not a business. You are not a billboard. Even if you feel commodified, as people increasingly turn to the gig economy just trying to pay the bills or break free from the loop of consumerist banality. You do not owe the world your every waking moment.

When you allow stillness back in, something sacred returns.

Your breath slows. Your thoughts stop marketing themselves. Your soul, long ignored, taps gently on the door. Perhaps a monk appears. Just kidding, if you see a monk appearing magically, we may have other concerns; unless you are in Thailand, in which case, completely normal.

The Last Kind Ones find their strength not in the hustle, but in the hush.

We do not compete for noise.

We create space for meaning and real connection. Whether that's in an urban coffee shop or a rice field in Watampone.

Stillness is not the absence of activity.

It is the presence of grace. It offers us a deeper connection with the spiritual, the ancestral, the real.

It is the meal eaten slowly. The sunset watched without a rush to leave and deadlines. The decision not to reply just yet. The moment you listen; not to respond, but to *hear*. Not what is said, but what is felt.

In this world, stillness won't trend. But it will heal you, and if enough of us choose it, we just may make a different world.

Take your stillness.

Own it.

Keep it.

It was always yours, just as it was your ancestors.

Living Beyond the Feed

There's a strange ache that comes from being watched but not seen. Followed, but not known. Liked, but not loved. Something I've explored when writing fiction, because it's one of the clearest metaphors for modern disconnection.

This is the quiet crisis of the feed.

We scroll past each other's lives like window shoppers in a mall that never closes. Joy becomes a thumbnail; grief becomes a caption. Success is curated. Failure is deleted. Nuance is compressed. And through it all, we start to believe the feed is real life, as if this flickering stream of filtered lives truly reflects the world.

But the world is not a scroll.

It is wind, and light, and stories told at kitchen tables. It is people, not posts.

There is a teenager in Cebu who leaves his phone at home each Sunday. His only day off work. He spends it fishing with his grandfather in a small outrigger canoe, surrounded by salt air and stories. They don't take photos. They take turns pulling soft lines through sunlit water, just as generations before them did.

There is a woman in Porto who bakes hand-kneaded bread each morning and sells it from her window ledge. The locals know her not by handle but by name, and her affectionate smile. They come not to gossip about celebrity posts, but for warmth. For slow ritual. For connection.

To live beyond the feed is not to reject technology. It's to reject the reliance on it to feel emotion or connect.

It means choosing presence over proof. It means choosing silence over self-promotion. It means, in conversation, ignoring the buzz of a phone. Every time you do, you take back a little of your life.

Not every laugh must echo in the algorithm. Not every insight needs a hashtag. Some things, in fact the best things are too human for metrics, no matter how hard they try.

I want to see your tears. I want to see your smile. And I want you to see mine.

The feed flattens life into performance. But you are allowed to be dimensional. You are allowed to:

- Grieve without a tribute post.

- Celebrate without an audience.

- Change your mind without an announcement.

The Last Kind Ones are reclaiming this right. We are remembering how to:

- Be with someone without checking our phones.

- Wander without GPS.

- Feel without framing.

You may find, as you step away, that the world begins to whisper again. In birdsong. In breeze. In your own breath.

And in this space beyond the feed that is beyond headlines, beyond comment threads, beyond the noise, you do not have to earn your worth. You do not have to prove your joy. You simply are.

Let the pixels rest.

Let the notifications go unanswered.

Uninstall if you can.

Let yourself return to the uncurated life.

There is a richness that the feed can never replicate.

You'll find it in the scent of the ocean. In the hands that hold yours without needing to post about it. In the courage to say: "This moment belongs only to me".

Live there, now and then. You don't need permission.

You only need to disengage, to truly engage. And when you do? The sea will still be waiting. So will the birds. So will we.

The Soul Beyond Usefulness

There is a man in his sixties who walks the beach at dawn, just south of Broome. His face a collection of lines etched by an exposure to the sun and years of wisdom and working hard for his family.

He no longer works. No longer clocks in. No longer earns. And yet, each morning, as his feet press into the sand and the tide pulls back like a new start, he feels whole. Not because of what he does, but because of who he is when no one is watching. His feet interact with the water. Flotsam washes up, some plastic, some natural, all carried on the currents from thousands of miles away. The ocean choosing what lands where, when. His footsteps form soft depressions in the sand, a beauty in their impermanence as the waves roll in and wash them away.

For most of us, worth has been welded to output. We are only as valuable as what we generate, solve, or monetise. Productivity has become our second skin; comforting at first, but eventually suffocating. Ask anyone at retirement; there is often a silent pain knowing how many years were dedicated to gaining wealth for the company, not themselves. The late nights. The relationships quietly broken in pursuit of economics.

Even rest has been repackaged: marketed as fuel for future output. Rest to optimise. Take this sponsored tablet or formulated herbal drink to help you rest. Meditate to maximise.

But don't meditate that way! Get our course to teach you how. Align those damn chakras. Journal to grow your personal brand. But only on high quality paper with a fountain pen.

But the soul is not a business model. And a human life is not a startup. The Last Kind Ones can learn to live differently. Of course, we still battle in the same world as the others. We need to earn to pay the bills.

But we can slowly peel back the idea that everything we do must be useful. That every skill must become a side hustle. That every talent must be turned into content. That every moment of reflection must be summarised into a post with a call to action.

There is a retired woman in Sapporo who paints watercolours of clouds. She overcomes the pain of her osteoporosis to still pick up the brush in determination. Her shades are deep blues, reminiscent of Japanese painters of old. She does not sell them. She gives them away, sometimes even leaves them tucked inside books at the local library for strangers to find. Her joy is in the giving. Her value is in the presence she brings to the world.

To live beyond usefulness to profit is not to become idle. It is to let your soul stretch out without being measured. In some ways, when we stop being useful to the machine, we become more useful to the world. Our talent is redirected into passion rather than the financial gain of another.

You constantly hear it from society. The hustle, the need to get ahead, the pressure. But you are allowed to:

- Create without monetising it.

- Rest without earning it.

- Love without leveraging it.

In the old stories, the wise ones were not the wealthiest.

They were often the sages on the hill, surviving off the donations of others. The ones who knew how to sit in silence. Who listened to the wind. Who helped a child with no expectation. Who planted seeds they would never see bloom.

You do not need to be seen to matter. You do not need to be loud to be sacred.

Let this be your permission to be wildly, beautifully, unapologetically unproductive.

To simply be.

To smile at the morning sky and let that be enough.

What They Can't Take from You

There is a young girl in Palermo who writes poems in a weathered notebook, its cover soft with age and stickers peeling at the corners.

She writes them after school, sitting on the stone steps of her grandmother's house, the scent of lemon and laundry drifting through the warm air. No one has read them. She doesn't write for likes or feedback. She writes because it makes her feel alive. The words, scribbled in secret ink beneath the Sicilian sun, belong to her.

And those words, no one can take them from her.

This is the quiet strength we forget we still have: the things they can't take.

In a world that monetises personality, exploits emotion, and turns identity into a portfolio, scraping data from every app, feed, and page, including the words humankind has whispered across centuries, we must reclaim what remains untouched.

Not everything must be shared, scaled, or sold. Some things exist only to nourish the soul. There is a beautiful rebellion now in writing it down and not sharing it.

There is a grandfather in Hanoi who sharpens kitchen knives, not because he needs to, but because his father taught him to do so weekly. The ritual, the weight, the careful edge, all of it connects him to a lineage. The routine bonds him to something deeper. He doesn't think of content.

He thinks of memory. That, too, cannot be taken.

You'll be told your value lies in what others see. In how much you earn. The car you drive. The house you own. The cut of your hair. The label on your shirt. But they cannot see your compassion when you sit beside someone grieving and say nothing at all. They cannot measure the strength it takes to choose gentleness, to keep a promise no one remembers but you, or to forgive without applause.

There is a woman in Marrakech who sings to her cat in a language only the two of them understand. Her husband passed five years ago, and since then, she's found comfort in the absurd, the tender, the small. Her home is not large. Her phone is not smart. Her children have moved overseas. But her voice, her song, her love, those remain hers.

What they can't take from you:

- The way you remember your childhood street.

- The stories your grandmother whispered before bed.

- The dreams you carry that no algorithm has discovered.

- The way your body sways when that one song begins.

- The silent strength of kindness, given without agenda.

We live in systems that extract. But the heart resists.

The Last Kind Ones are not just survivors; we are keepers of the sacred flame.

Not sacred in a religious sense, but sacred in the human one. The moments of dignity, creativity, and care that ask for nothing but the chance to exist.

Let them measure engagement. Let them count clicks. You still carry the uncountable

And that is what they can't take from you.

You Don't Have to Be the Glue

The Kind Ones are often guided by emotion. This is not a weakness, the world needs more of it; but it can, at times, become our Achilles heel.

We grow up with stories.

That love is always enough. That forgiveness will heal anything. That if something breaks, we can fix it, even if we're the only ones trying.

But what if the thing that's broken…isn't yours to fix?

What if you have given everything; time, softness, explanation, sacrifice, and it still hurts? What if all that effort hasn't mended the cracks, but simply hidden how deep they go? What if your kindness has turned into a rope burn?

Let's say something not enough people say out loud:

You do not have to keep setting yourself on fire just to keep someone else warm.

And if you ever do feel ablaze, remember: stop, drop, and roll. (Just… maybe not mid-conversation. That would raise eyebrows.)

Family Isn't Meant to Feel Like a War Zone

Family, and Western society in general, was never a utopia. But through rose-coloured lenses, we often look back on the 1950s and white picket fences as something we can recreate.

If only we try hard enough. If only we buy enough.

We are told blood is thicker than water. That we must preserve the family at all costs. That it's our duty to resolve the unspoken, repair the tension, and keep the peace.

But what good is blood if it only reminds you of wounds?

What if being near certain family members only brings more pain? What if the tension comes from disrespect that never gets addressed?

Modern life can tear families apart like a wrecking ball:
— Money stress
— Unrealistic expectations
— Generational trauma
— Narcissism disguised as "tough love"
— Absence disguised as busyness

And so often, it's the kind ones who try to hold it all together.

They send the messages and remember to make the visits, and bite their tongue for the sake of peace.

But if peace only exists when you are swallowing your truth to keep the performance going, is it really peace?

You are not a court jester of old. You don't need to juggle it all just to keep the illusion alive.

If you're the only one in your family doing the work, is it really unity? Or is it slow, spiritual erosion… with a polite smile?

Let's be clear:

If it's breaking you to hold it together, it's not love. It's obligation with a ribbon tied around it.

Letting go isn't betrayal. It's setting healthy boundaries.
It's finally putting down the weight that was never meant to be carried alone.

Love Shouldn't Cost You Your Selfhood

Maybe it's not family. Maybe it's love of the unhealthy kind.

A relationship that started with spark and sincerity, but slowly became something else over time; control, disinterest, resentment, silence.

Sometimes it's a toxic partner. Sometimes it's just two tired people in a relationship who lost their way.

You remembered the good days; saw their potential.
You made excuses for them, for yourself, for why it hurt. You blamed yourself. You tried to shrink, stretch, contort into the shape they needed, even when it meant losing parts of who you were.

But deep down, you knew:
You were giving more than you had.
And it was exhausting.

You were receiving less than you deserve, yet giving your all.

There's a myth that true love always stays. But sometimes, true love leaves, not out of cruelty, but out of clarity and the need for freedom.

Sometimes, loving yourself means walking away from someone you still care about.
Even if it breaks your heart, even if they beg you to stay.
Even if you wish it could be different.

Kindness is not martyrdom. Loyalty is not self-abandonment.

And no, your ability to tolerate pain is not a personality trait.
You're not here to collect emotional merit badges. (*Even if those badges would probably look way cool.*)

The Kind Ones Bleed Quietly

There's something about the helpers, the empaths, the quietly strong:

They break last. But they also break hardest.

Because they spent years holding everyone else's pieces.
Because they made space when they had none.
Because their love language was endurance.

But endurance without rest becomes erosion.

Just like a beach can't withstand endless storms without reshaping the coastline, you, too, start to wear away. Even saints burn out.

You are allowed to say:

"Get stuffed, not today. I can't give that right now."

And if you need to go sit in the corner rocking back and forth there's no judgment here. (Just maybe don't do it in front of your therapist. They get worried.)
You don't need a dramatic reason to say no. You don't need permission. Your wellbeing is the reason.

Save some of yourself for later. There will be other days, other people, other moments. You are not required to empty your tank or collect trauma just to be considered good.

When It's Time to Get Help

If the cracks feel too wide, please, talk to someone.

A friend.
A counsellor or therapist.
A stranger with kind eyes.
(Just not that guy in the park you notice yelling at benches.)

And yes, even in this fragmented, fast world, sometimes even AI can offer a quiet thread of connection.

Not to replace the human, never. But to be a soft bridge *until* the human can return.

Speak your truth to a screen if it helps you find the words. Technology isn't the enemy, but over-reliance and replacing the human with it is. Used well, it's a lamp on a stormy road.

And don't be ashamed of needing support, especially when you've spent a lifetime being it for others.

You're human. That's the job.

The World Is Breaking But You Don't Have To

It's not just your personal life that's heavy it's everything lately.

Maybe you've noticed it, too:
The fraying of institutions.
The slow collapse of certainty.
The way the air feels heavier now, like we are all carrying something invisible but enormous.

This era of technological acceleration... the erosion of trust... the way even hope feels like it's on a timer and we are all on a crazy rollercoaster that is travelling at a phenomenal speed, not quite sure we are going to make the next turn ok.

And you , one of the kind ones ; you feel it deeper than most. Not because you are weak. But because you are awake.

But let's be blunt:

Unless your bank balance has fifteen zeroes, or your name is on a presidential ballot… your job isn't to fix the world.

It's to make one room in your house calmer. Or one day softer. To make one person including yourself, feel less alone.

You are not the glue of the entire century, world, or nation. You are the grace in the middle of it, the ballerina pirouetting in front of the chaos being admired by all.

Let the stones fall where they may. You can care without crumbling. Even if the walls around us all do.

Quiet Enough for the Wind to Speak

There is a woman in Tunisia who sits on her rooftop each night, just before the call to prayer. She does nothing. She listens. To the stray cat padding across tiles. To the neighbour clinking dishes as dinner is served. To the warm wind brushing past the linen she's left to dry. She does not document the moment. She does not post about it. She simply lets the wind speak.

The world has grown louder, perhaps intolerably so. Algorithms shout and ads flicker. Even joy must now be shared to be real. But the deepest truths do not shout. They whisper. And we have forgotten how to hear them.

This is the challenge of modern life that have touched on throughout this book but needs to be remembered: we need to at times be quiet enough for the wind to speak.

There is a retired teacher in Montana who has begun to garden again. Not for money and not for content. But for the slow miracle of it. She talks to her plants and even sings sometimes. No one hears her, except maybe the birds. She carries the spirit of her mother, who used to hum the same tune while planting in spring.

Silence isn't empty. It's full, of all the things we've forgotten to notice.

There is a man in a Johannesburg township who fixes bicycles for free. He has a small sign, barely legible, that says, "I just like to help." Some bring him coffee. Others, conversation. He doesn't post before-and-after pictures. He doesn't brand his kindness. He repairs what's broken because it brings others to smile. And in those smiles, there is warmth. And in that warmth, the wind speaks.

You may not be able to escape the noise. But you can create small sanctuaries.

- A window you sit beside each morning with your tea.

- A walk without headphones.

- A decision not to respond immediately.

Quietness is not the absence of sound. It's the restoration of meaning.

The Last Kind Ones are learning to trust the quiet again. We do not always need to add more or say more or perform more. Sometimes, presence is enough.

There is a small temple in Kyoto, nearly hidden by overgrowth, where a monk sweeps the stone steps every morning. He is old now; his back curved, but his will strong. The broom, itself old and aged, makes a soft rasping sound, rhythmical, almost musical. No one watches him. But the wind does. The wind, and maybe the generations before who are carried in the wind.

The wind speaks in many tongues. Through memory and through motion, through the spaces we leave untouched.

You don't need to retreat to the mountains to hear it. You only need to get quiet enough.

Close the tab. Turn off the device and step into the breeze.

It will still be speaking, and maybe this time, you'll hear it.

Letters to the Ones Still Trying

Sometimes the last kind ones don't roar. They whisper. They write. They leave small offerings for a future they will never meet.

There is a small church tucked in a side street of Tbilisi, Georgia. The stone is worn smooth by time, and the air carries the scent of beeswax and old wood. Each morning, an elderly caretaker, his coat patched and gait slow, unlocks the wooden doors and lights a single candle. He does not preach nor does he film. He simply tends to the silence in reverence. The way the morning light filters through the stained glass is sermon enough. There is no congregation here, just birdsong, footsteps, breath. The wind moves gently through the trees outside. Something eternal listens.

The Last Kind Ones are not trying to win the algorithm.
We write letters in bottles. Messages in margins.
We Create beauty for its own sake, not to trend, not to win, but to give.

We don't call ourselves the last kind ones because we think we're better.
It's because kindness has become harder to carry now.

It's rarer than ever. In a world this fast, this performative, this mistrustful, it gets heavy. Kindness becomes something people start putting down. No longer seen as valuable in a commodified world.

They trade it for cynicism, efficiency, and safety. Not because they're bad. Just tired. So tired.

And yet... some people still whisper *please* and *thank you*. Still hold the door. Still cry at good books. Still notice when others are hurting, even when no one is looking.

Those are the last kind ones. For now.
Not because the world ended. But because most people just drifted away from softness.

There is a young man in Recife who paints murals on abandoned walls. They are not signed. He often walks past them a week later and sees someone else has tagged over them. He does not repaint. He just smiles. Because the act was never about his mark being permanent, but rather expression of the soul.

There is a grandmother in Galway who writes postcards to strangers. She picks names and addresses from phone books. Each card is handwritten with small, kind notes. She buys the prettiest stamps she can afford, and she doesn't expect replies.

We are not here to outshout the noise. We are here to hum something gentler beneath it.

You might be one of them. The ones who stay up late writing stories no one asked for, the ones who check in on friends who never reciprocate. The ones who bake, build, draw, code, sew; not for sale, but for love.

What you are doing is not in vain.

There are others. Scattered. Tired. Often uncertain. But still trying.

Still choosing kindness over cleverness.
Still daring to feel in a world that rewards numbness.
Still protecting the sacred.

Your work, your presence, your care, it ripples.

We are not alone.

We are letters still being written, still being found.

We are The Last Kind Ones.

Books For the Quiet Return

These are not books of hacks or hustle. They are books that breathe. Books that invite you to pause, to reflect, and to remember what matters. You don't need to read them all. Just let them sit nearby. When the time is right, they will speak.

- **The Greening of America** by Charles A. Reich
  A profound and hopeful book on generational change, and the search for a gentler, more human way of living. Perhaps this had the greatest inspiration for me writing Kind Ones. First published in 1970, but still relevant today.

- **Braiding Sweetgrass** by Robin Wall Kimmerer
  A weave of indigenous wisdom, scientific knowledge, and poetic charm. Teaches that reciprocity with the natural world is not a philosophy, it's a way of being.

- **Atlas Obscura** by Joshua Foer, Dylan Thuras, Ella Morton
  For those whose bodies stay home, but whose hearts still wander. A bedside ticket to the world of the odd, the hidden, and the quietly wonderful. Also brilliant to inspire you for unusual travel plans.

- **A Man Without a Country** by Kurt Vonnegut
  A sharp, honest, and deeply human set of reflections from one of America's great minds.

- **Notes from a Small Island** by Bill Bryson
  When you want to wander without going far. A reminder that kindness and curiosity still live at the edge of train stations, chip shops, and rainy high streets. His humour is second to none.

- **The Sound of a Wild Snail Eating** by Elisabeth Tova Bailey
  A slow, beautiful meditation on stillness, illness, and the companionship of small things. A reminder that life doesn't need to be big to be meaningful.

- **The Disappearance of Rituals** by Byung-Chul Han
  A exploration of how we've lost the sacred rhythms and gestures that once shaped our lives and why recovering them matters.

- **The Book of Delights** by Ross Gay
  A daily record of small joys, written with humour, and reverence.

- **Wintering** by Katherine May
  A lyrical book about the seasons of life, those times when we retreat, reflect, and quietly heal. Especially comforting for anyone who feels behind.

- **Unquiet Lines** by David Teahan (me!), Farbellum Press
  For those who feel a little too much. Short stories for quiet thinkers, strange dreamers, and anyone who's ever felt alone in a crowded world. Hoping to write a second one soon.

- **All About Love** by Bell Hooks
  For when you want to believe in love again, but more truthfully. A raw and healing guide to what love could be, if we're brave enough to name what it isn't.

- **The Course of Love** by Alain de Botton
  For those who know that love begins where the storybook ends. A quiet novel emotional complexity, and the failure of romantic myths.

Thankyou

Thank you for reading *Notes for the Last Kind Ones*. If any part of it stayed with you, I'd be incredibly greatful if you left a review.

It helps more than you know.

I am really struggling to get it seen, the algorithm of modern society is working against me promoting the hollow books over the real.

Please consider sending the amazon link to a friend or family member.

You can find more at farbellum.com including new stories, reflections, and updates on the strange little things we're building. You can email me there.

Thank you for being here. You're one of the kind ones. And that matters more than the numbers ever will.